"I want to be known as a wife, a mother, a grandmother. That's what I am. And I'd like to be known as someone who really cared about people and worked very, very hard to make America more literate."

– Barbara Bush

Design by Dietz Associates Inc., Kennebunk, Maine

Copyright © 2018 Kennebunkport Conservation Trust
All rights reserved. Published 2018.
Printed in the United States of America by Penmor Lithographers, Lewiston, Maine.

This book may not be reproduced, in whole or in part, in any form (beyond that copying permitted by Sections 107 and 108 of the U.S. Copyright Law and except by reviewers for the public press), without written permission from the publisher. Requests for permission should be addressed by email to *info@kctoffice.org* or in writing to The Kennebunkport Conservation Trust, PO Box 7004, Cape Porpoise, Maine 04014.

www.kporttrust.org

ISBN 978-0-9774943-2-3

Copyright © 2018 Kennebunkport Conservation Trust

OUR BELOVED BARBARA

MEMORIES OF A COMMUNITY

Kennebunkport Conservation Trust, 57 Gravelly Brook Road, Kennebunkport, ME 04046
Mailing address: PO Box 7004, Cape Porpoise, ME 04014
207.967.3465   info@kctoffice.org

The first time that President Bush and Barbara came back to Kennebunkport after George won the election, I was in the Port Hardware Store when all of these cars started to arrive. Then Barbara came in with a couple of Secret Service agents. I was standing close by when she turned to me and said in a somber voice, "Poor George, he will probably never be able to walk the Kennebunkport streets alone again." I can't remember my response, but I think I said, "That's what happens when you become the President of the United States."

– Carolyn Broad (Maden)

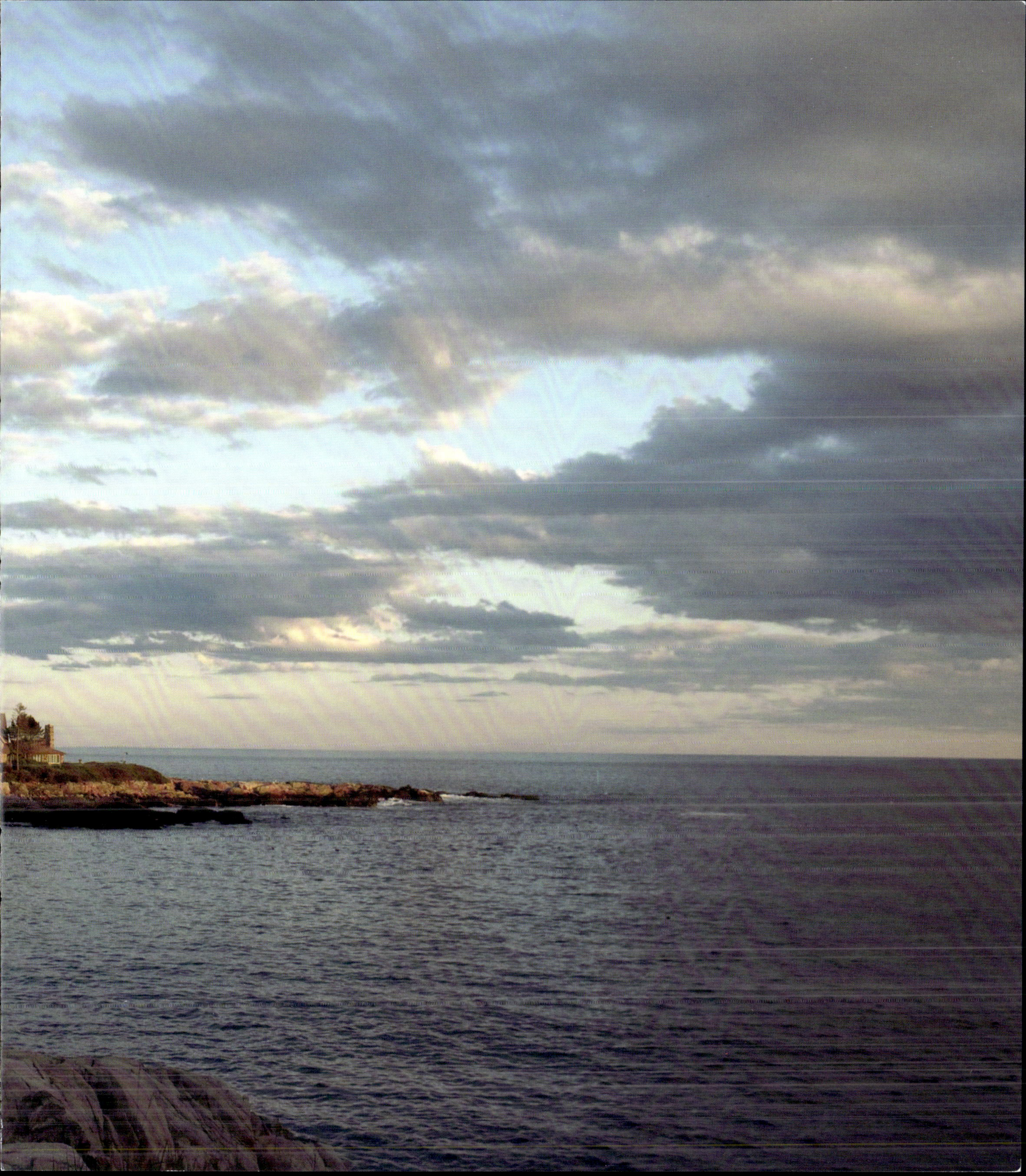

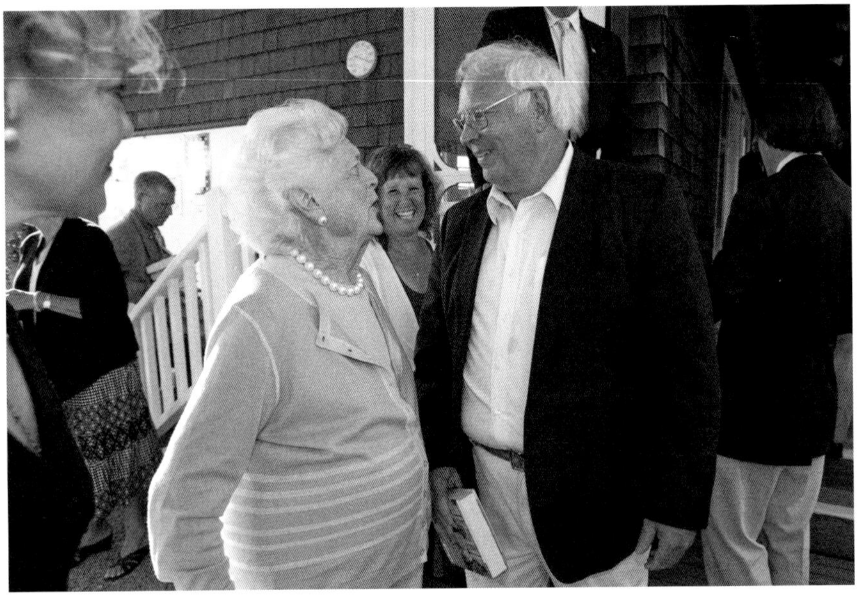

FOREWORD

We at the Kennebunkport Conservation Trust were deeply saddened by the passing of Barbara Pierce Bush. The nation knew her as a beloved First Lady, with a warm smile, keen wit and the caring forthrightness of a grandmother. She was known for her tireless work for a more literate America and her steadfast belief in the benefits of volunteerism. That, after all, was the way she lived her life, a willing worker and advocate for cancer research, the homeless, the elderly, AIDS understanding and prevention and better schools. In Kennebunkport, we were blessed to also know her as a friend and neighbor. We could see first hand her deep love and devotion to her husband, family and those around her. We witnessed the joy she derived from her garden, her dogs and her community. For George and Barbara Bush, Kennebunkport was their "Anchor to Windward", a place to play and pray and tighten the bonds of family and friendships. It was a place where love could be freely given and received, a place to relax from the burdens of a nation, a place to build up resources needed to meet the challenges ahead. We saw Barbara at the local market, at the library, walking the dog on the beach, even in the aisles of Wal-Mart. She was always patient, caring and gracious. We saw her wonderful humor, her generosity, her basic kindness, her decency. She was one of us, and she had earned our love, respect and admiration. May God bless you Barbara. Our lives were made richer for having shared a bit of your journey.

– **Tom Bradbury**
Executive Director
Kennebunkport Conservation Trust

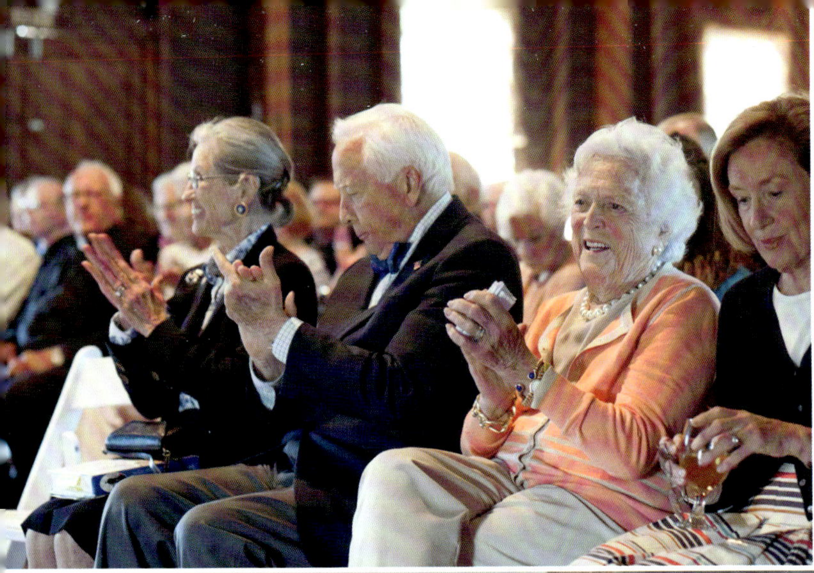

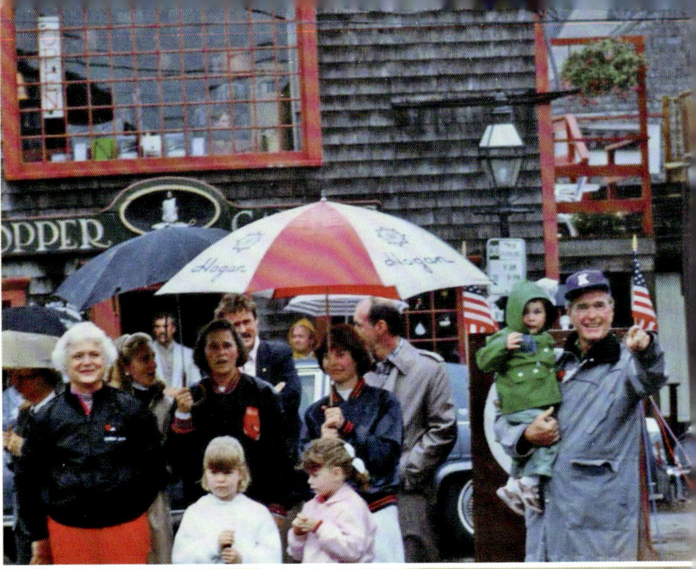

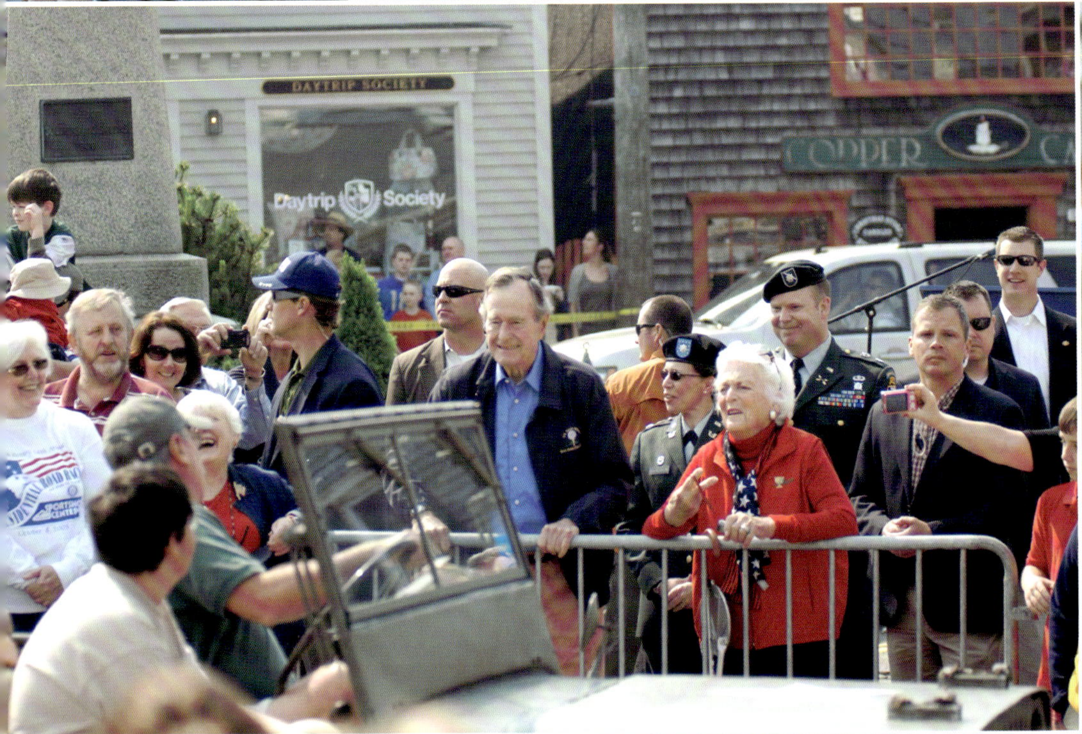
DAYTRIP SOCIETY
Daytrip Society

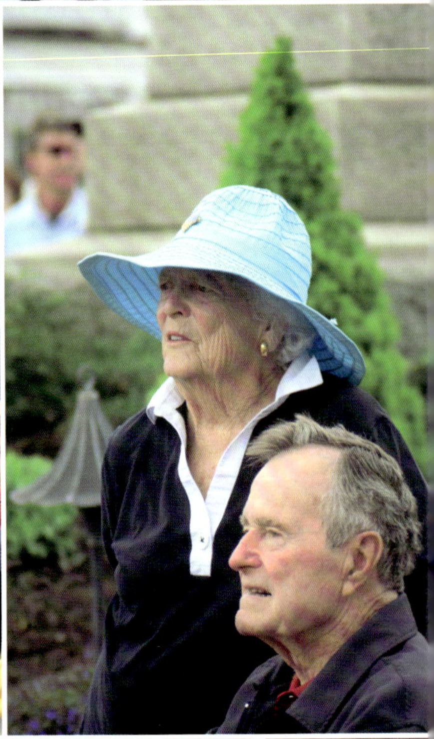

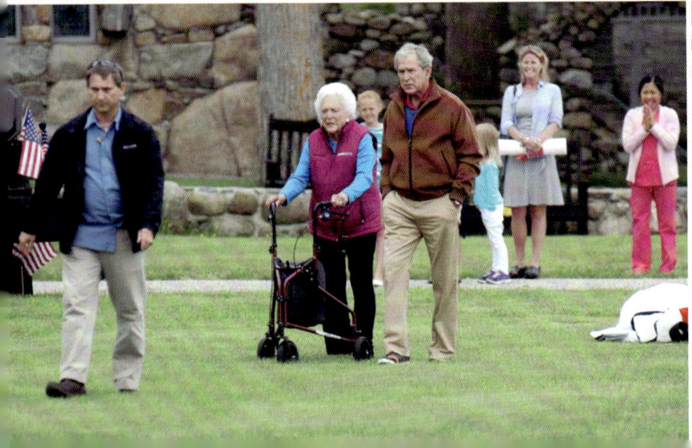

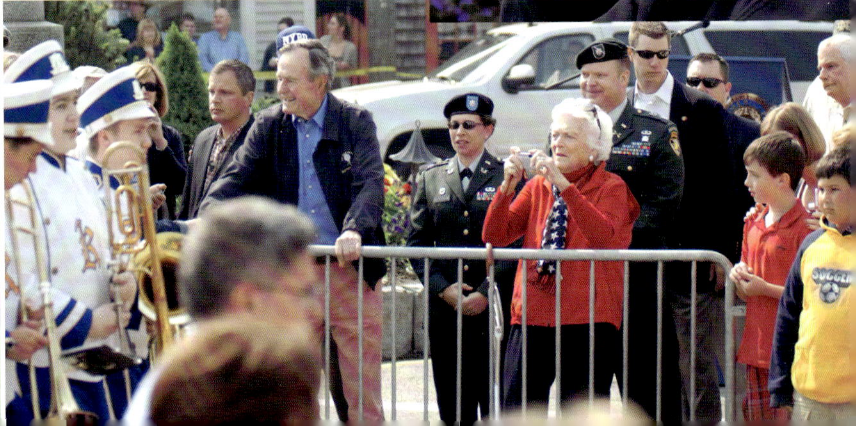
SOCCER

OUR TOWN

"Like you, we love Kennebunkport with a passion. I love the people, the ocean, the beaches, my 'Ganny's Garden.' All of it."

– **Barbara Bush**

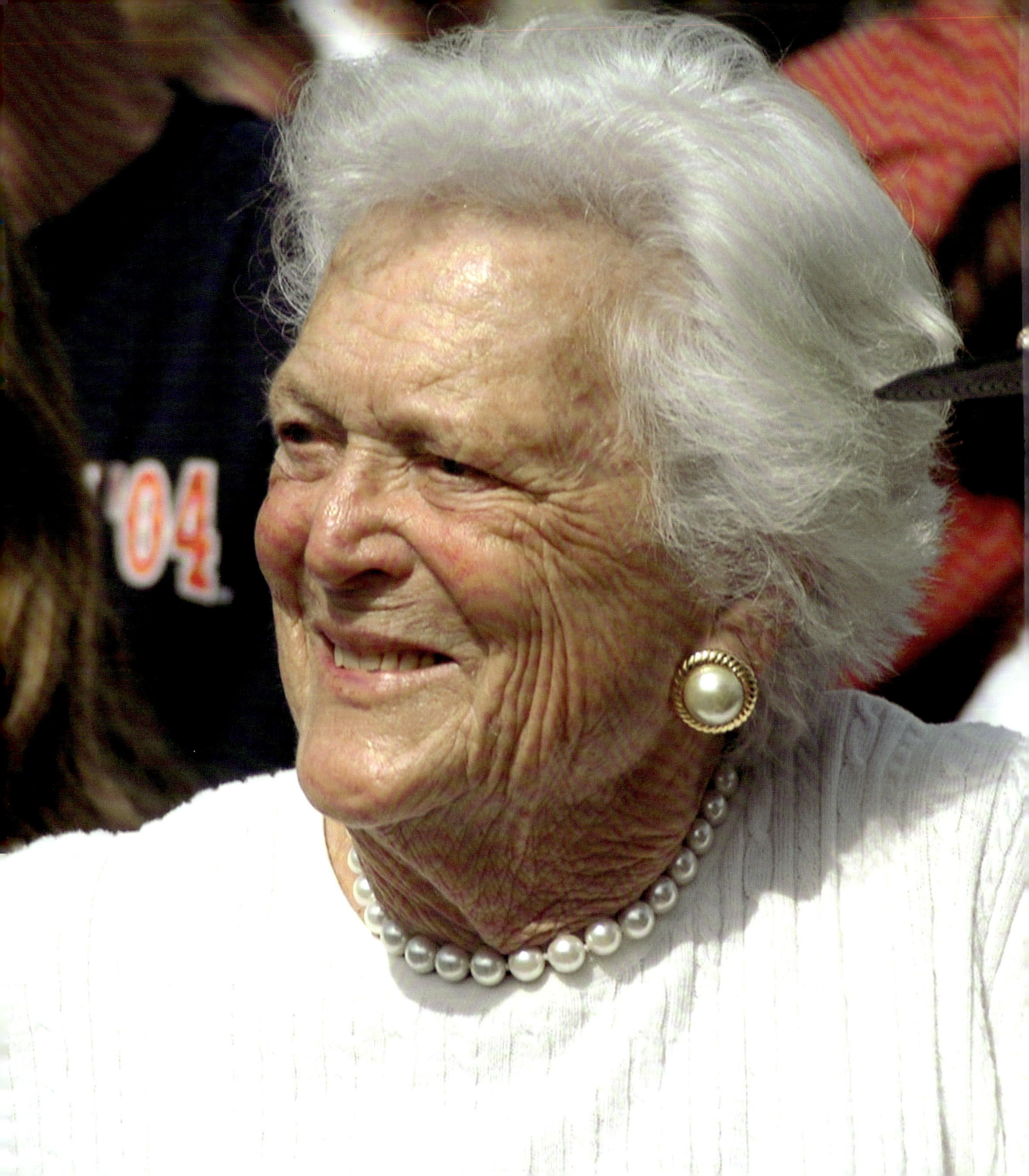

A TRIBUTE

Ganny's Garden, given by friends and loved ones of Barbara Pierce Bush, is a lovely spot to rest and reflect near downtown Kennebunkport. There you'll find, on a sculpted bench, a wide brim sunhat — the kind Barbara wore in her garden — and an open copy, face down, of her favorite book, Jane Austen's *Pride and Prejudice*.

Though I am taking the quote slightly out of context, because the one who spoke it was pretentiously touting her love of reading — nonetheless, Jane Austen used one of her characters in that book to utter a wonderful truth, "I declare…there is no enjoyment like reading! How much sooner one tires of anything than of a book!" There was nothing pretentious about Barbara Bush. She loved reading and literacy — for all — and this was Barbara Bush's great passion.

Every great book has a good beginning — but also a wonderful end. And so, the life story of Barbara Bush is best described as the consummate "good read."

She was a friend to people of every political persuasion, race, and religion. Her generosity of spirit did not draw lines that kept others out; hers was a life of circles that sought to bring others in. The least of Barbara's virtues was patience. If you were sharing a meal, or waiting on her favorite drink (Bourbon and water, for the record), and things were slowing up, she would ask "Why the holdup?"

My guess is that she has already hunted down Jane Austen and has said, "Well, how did things turn out with Mr. Darcy and Elizabeth Bennett?" Or, knowing Barbara as we all do, she may be telling Jane how things should have turned out.

In the meantime, until each of our time comes, she would want us to carry on… to live as she lived — fully, deeply. To laugh, and laugh often. To love all that God sends our way. And to serve one another, the common good, and especially the purposes of God.

The Reverend Dr. Russell J. Levenson, Jr.
Extracted from his Homily for Barbara Pierce Bush, April 21, 2018

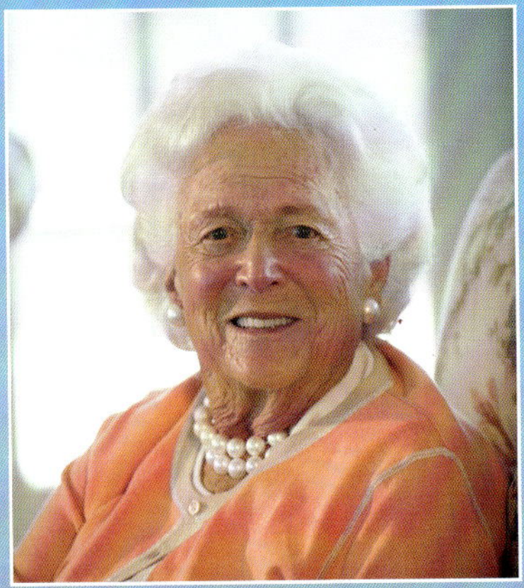
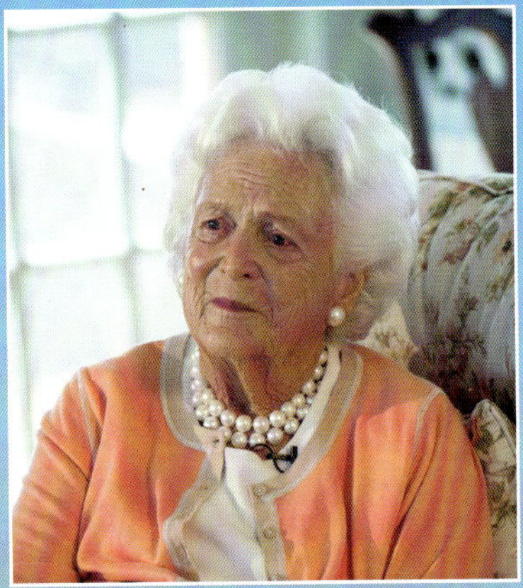
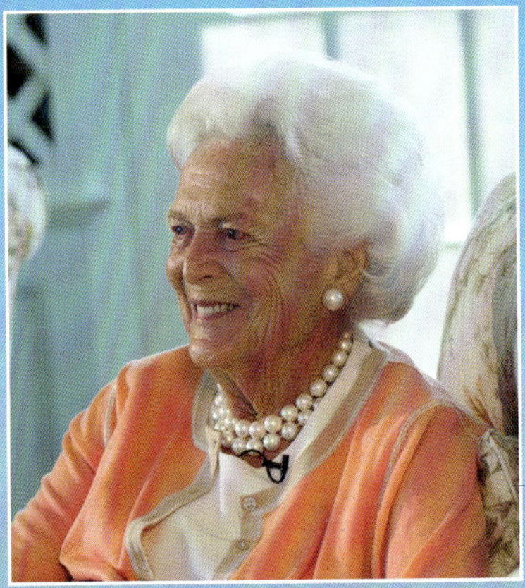
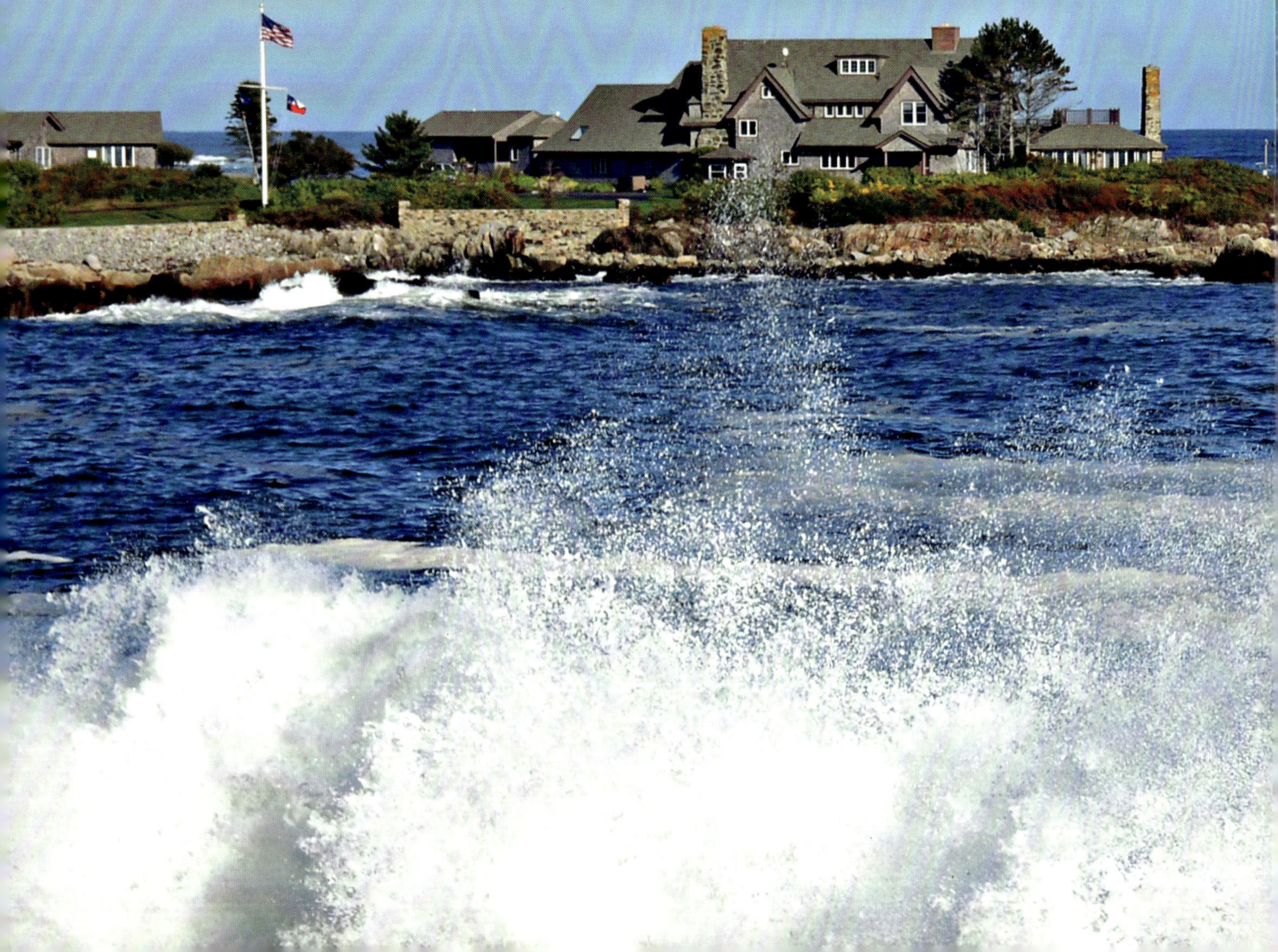

"My beloved Barbara and I go to sleep in our bedroom
literally a stone's throw from the sea.
We can hear the pounding of the ocean waves when
the ocean is angry and strong; and we can hear the gentle murmurs
of that same sea when all is calm.
I can feel all this in the fiber of my soul."
– George H. W. Bush

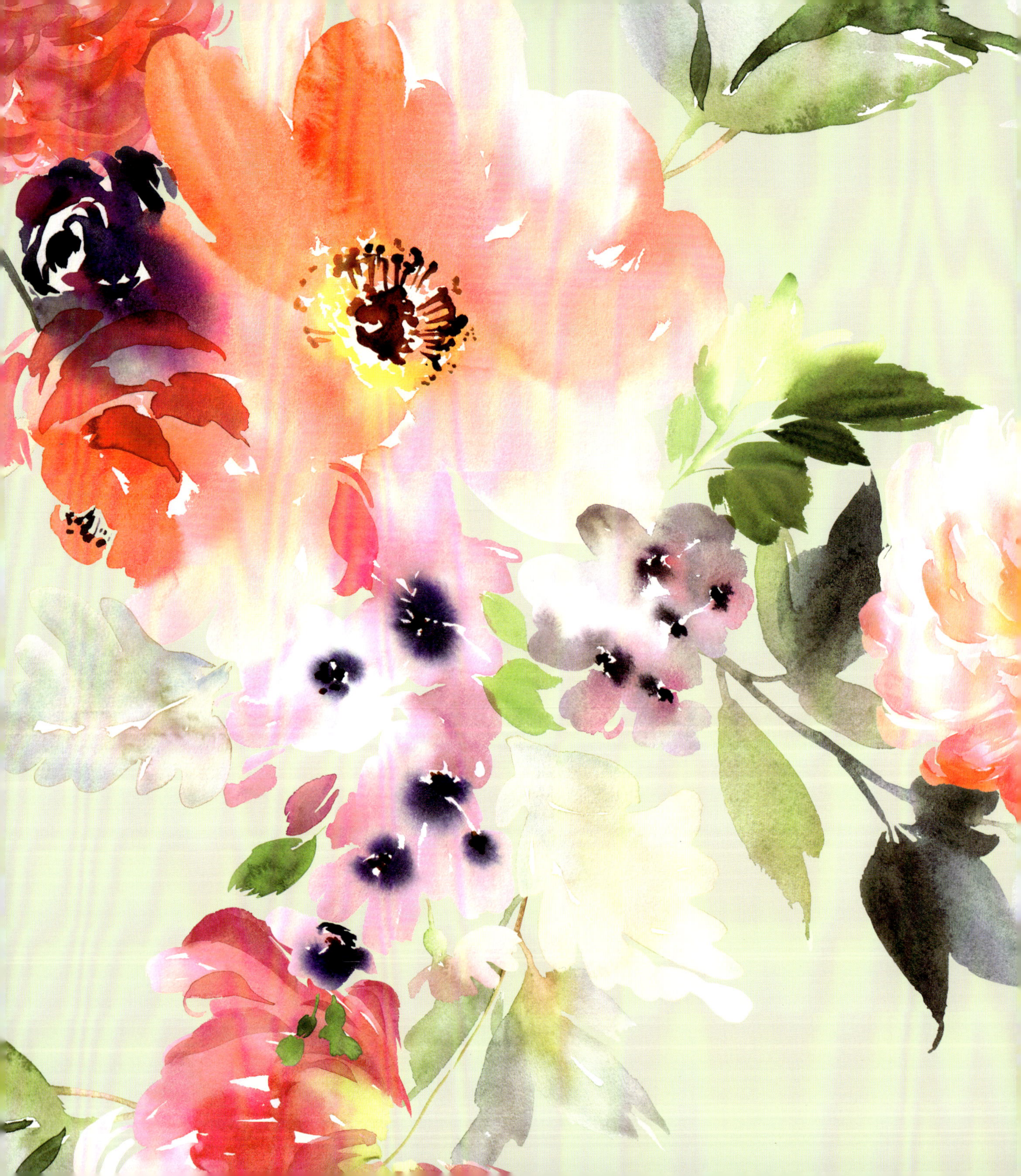

AMONG FRIENDS

✢

"At the end of your life, you will never regret not having passed one more test, not winning one more verdict or not closing one more deal. You will regret time not spent with a husband, a friend, a child, or a parent."
— **Barbara Bush**

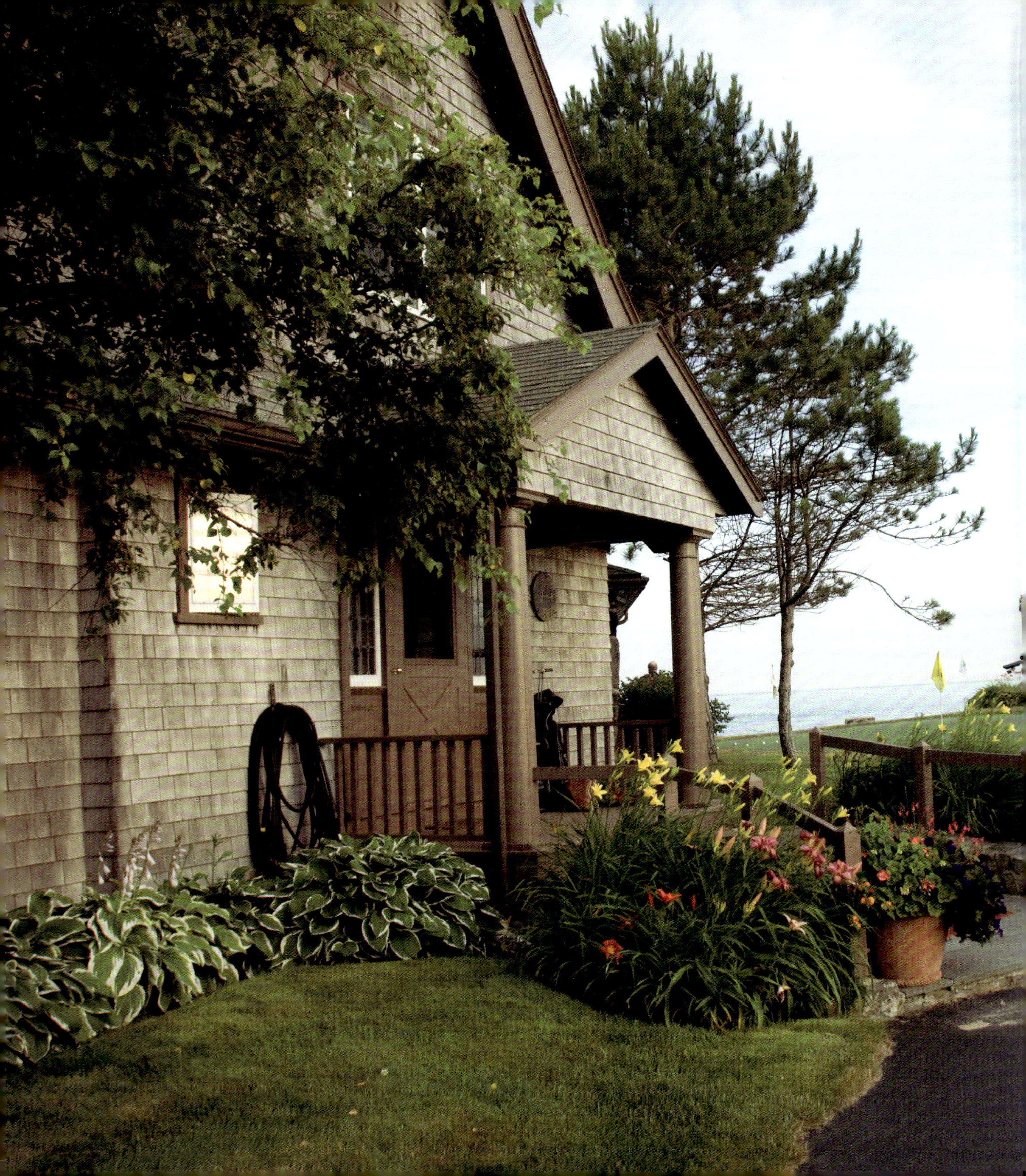

When she heard I was coming to Houston to visit Linda Casey, Barbara called Linda when she and the President got back to Houston and said, "Carolyn is coming to Houston for a few days to visit you and you MUST come to visit me." We did, and had a great time together, talking about everything. I left with four signed Millie books and a nice memory that will last a lifetime — until Barbara and I meet again in our Heavenly Home.

— **Carolyn Broad (Maden)**

As a tennis professional, my husband would from time to time be invited to join the Bush family in a competitive match. I would go with him, joining Barbara on the sidelines to cheer everyone on. During the course of the game she'd talk with great affection about her grandchildren, gardens and happenings around town. She would also want to know all about my young son, Houston. She was a most gracious and real woman who adored her family. This would include her puppies. I feel blessed to have known her. — **Lesa Kraft Angelos**

I make custom wooden jigsaw puzzles under the name of *Bogarts Wooden Jigsaw Puzzles*. I knew for years that Mrs. Bush loved playing with wooden jigsaw puzzles. I wanted Mrs. Bush to have one of my puzzles so I was able to get a wonderful puzzle into the hands of one of her Secret Service agents who in turn delivered it to Mrs. Bush. I never expected to get a response, and to my amazement, I received a handwritten note from Mrs. Bush several days later expressing her surprise and delight with what I had given her. Over the next five years, we developed a friendship. During that time I created ten more jigsaw puzzles for her family that she thoroughly enjoyed. With every puzzle I made for her, I received a beautiful handwritten note. Her notes were very thoughtful, always containing wit and wisdom.

When I explained to her how I mounted my puzzle images, she responded in a note: "Fascinating that you are printing now right on the wood. Makes sense in a world where making sense is needed!"

The last time she requested a puzzle, she wanted to feature a photo of her cherished dogs Mini and Bibi. With a note on her personal notepaper, Mrs. Bush included the image she wanted to use. After sending the puzzle to her, sure enough, I receive a note back. "I am thrilled with my new puzzle from *Bogarts*," she wrote.

"How thoughtful of you and how lucky I was that I wrote you on my best notepaper? I can't wait to put the puzzle out. I will pass it on to my puzzle making children." Her note included a hand-drawn smiley face.
 — **Jay Hollis**

At the Cape Arundel Golf Course dedication of the "41 House" I was chatting with a group of women, including Mrs. Bush. Jeb walked in and came over to his mother. She looked at him and said, "Go home and change your shirt!" So classic!
— Ronni Hass

For many years Mrs. Bush was an occasional visitor to my store. On one visit she arrived wearing somewhat eccentric footwear; one blue sneaker and one pink sneaker. Someone in the store questioned her mismatch. I paraphrase her memorable response.

"For some time I had been complaining to George about my inability to find a pair of old-fashioned, non-engineered sneakers. One day a package arrived on our doorstep filled with dozens of pairs of old fashioned KEDS sneakers, one pair of every color manufactured. I find now that I have to wear two colors on every outing in an effort to exhaust my entire wardrobe of colors."

I always enjoyed having Mrs. Bush as one of my customers.
— Dannah

I will always remember Mrs. Bush sharing with me one of her favorite authors, Elizabeth George, who wrote A GREAT DELIVERANCE. She was kind and treated us all like part of the family on our visits to Kennebunkport over the years and during a special "Summiteers" trip we made to Houston. I will never forget sitting in her home admiring the rug that she made while traveling the world on Air Force One. The rug occasionally doubled as a pillow when in need of a little shuteye.

The Brazilian dinner and Secret Service escort provided yet another lifetime highlight. At times it feels like it was a dream. Mrs. Bush was a woman to be respected. The matriarch of her family, she was admired by all, and will be sorely missed.

– Jill Rudberg

I remember my children, so little, sitting at her feet at the Kennebunkport Graves Library, listening to her tell the story of *Ferdinand the Bull* with great spirit and animation. And at the former Arundel Barn Theater, I remember how kind the former First Lady was to my little girl when my daughter wanted to hand her a flower at intermission. Mrs. Bush said: "What a pretty flower. You should hold onto it. It's as pretty as you. Let's go meet the President." And off they went.

– Kirsten Camp

Several years ago, Mrs. Bush agreed to introduce author/historian David McCullough at the annual Graves Library fundraiser at the Kennebunk River Club. A few days prior to the event, she came by the Library to look around and talk to me about my job. "What did I like about my job?" she asked. "Everything," I replied. I told her about the kids, how we enjoyed reading to them, picking out the right books for them, and even singing and dancing with them at story time. We both agreed that there is nothing like the sound of children laughing. Nothing!

At the fundraiser a few days later, she stood up to introduce Mr. McCullough. Before she started talking about him, she spoke about her visit to the Library, her conversation with me, and the way my eyes "sparkled" when I talked about the children.

When I got home that night, my husband greeted me at the door and asked how everything went at the event. My response was "Mrs. Bush said I sparkled." I will never forget how she made me feel so very validated and grateful about my career as a Librarian.

What a wonderful role model, lover of all children, straight shooter, and funny human being.

– Mary-Lou Boucouvalas

At what became a tradition over the years, the President and Bar would come to our house for dinner prior to their departure back to Houston for the winter. One year while I was finishing up preparations for serving dinner, Bar wandered over to my china cabinet. After a few moments she called me over and inquired about four colorful, artistically painted glasses in the cabinet. I told her that they had been a present, but I hardly used them as I usually had more than four people for dinner. She laughed and said, "I have four of the same glasses and I never use them as we never have just four people for dinner." She and I chuckled about our beautiful useless glasses. Dinner was then ready and we all sat down for great food and wonderful company.

Two weeks later I received a package from Houston. Inside were Bar's four glasses and a note that read, "Now you can use them." She never missed a beat!

– Anne Raynor

WALKER'S POINT
KENNEBUNKPORT, MAINE

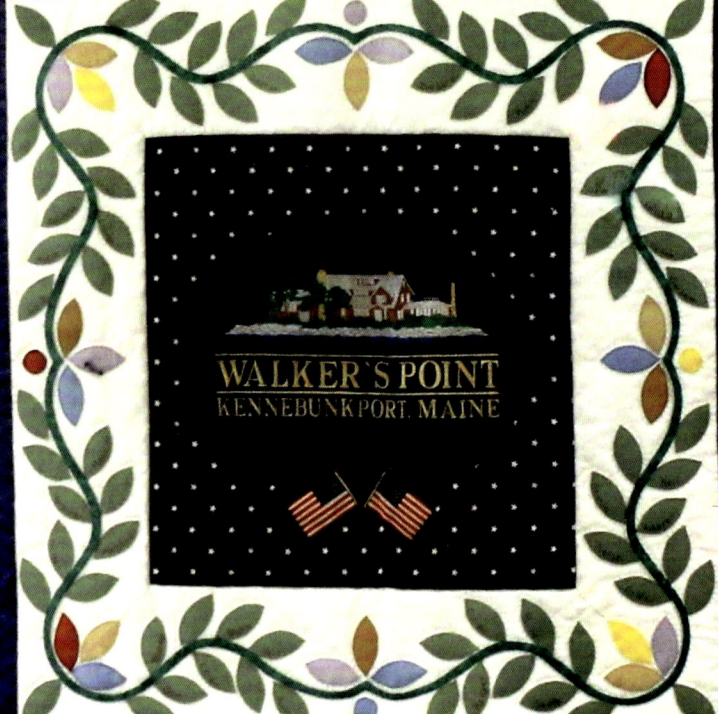

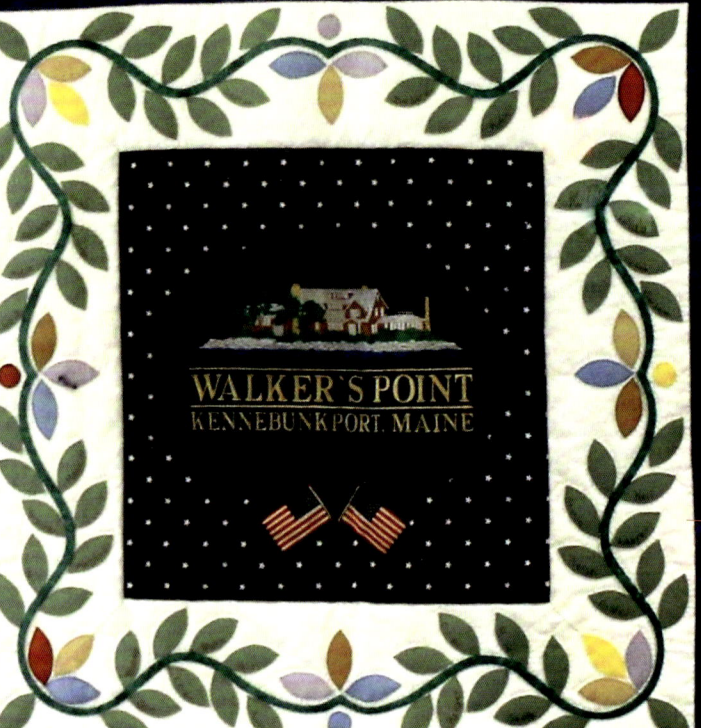

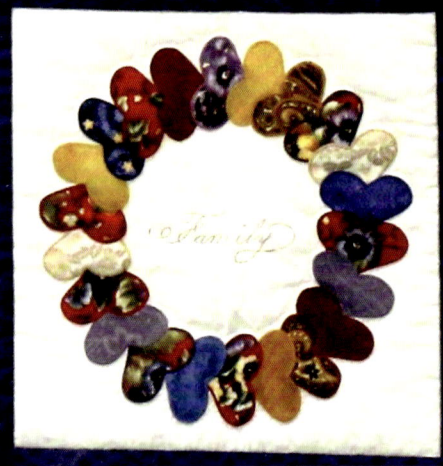

My husband Tom and I were invited to the celebration gathering for Mrs. Bush's 75th birthday. Although the invitation clearly read "no gifts," I felt uncomfortable with that. I wanted to do something special for a special lady. So I made her a quilt. During the weeks that preceded the event, Tom took over many of the household duties, allowing me time to conceive of a suitable pattern and then bring that design to life. With each completed block, and as the initials of every one of her children and grandchildren were added into the fabric, I became more and more excited. I wanted it to be a piece that I would be proud to present to Mrs. Bush, and one that she would be happy to receive. At her birthday party we left the wrapped quilt in a place we thought it would be found. Several days later I received a lovely note expressing her thanks and appreciation, even as she wondered where it could best be displayed.

Years later Tom and I were invited to attend the ten-year anniversary of the opening of the George H. W. Bush Presidential Library and Museum in College Station, Texas. While there, we received a call inviting us to the Bush's private quarters. Barbara wanted to show me where my gift had ended up. She led us from the living room, down the hall and there, just outside her office, was the quilt, beautifully installed and with a small "created by" plaque. What an honor!

— Shirley Bradbury

Many of us who knew, honored and loved Barbara Bush, especially those living as neighbors of the Bush family at Walker's Point, lament her loss after 93 years. I can never forget either of the Bushes at social gatherings. Whenever I happened to introduce new folks to each of them they were always congenial, happy to learn about our guests interests and plans. There was also plenty of good cheer! Barbara had great smiles for crowds of all sizes — many I remember well during a number of important community occasions when I had the honor of introducing her. I also remember other times when Barbara was riding with George and others in his almighty speedboat *Fidelity*, as they occasionally cruised up and down Cape Porpoise Harbor, including some smiling and waving to our Card family on shore. Very special times indeed! So now, at age 83, I wish I had written down a few notes on at least a "Bush" or two! They lived just a mile or so down from Cape Porpoise. Until her passing, Barbara managed to continue her busy and incredibly meaningful life with people of all ages and backgrounds. Now in my retirement from dentistry, I finally have more time to read Barbara's books and other writings, which radiate her significant legacy. . .from Houston and Kennebunkport.

– **Robert L. Card, DDS** *(retired)*

In the summer before she passed, Mrs. Bush visited Sandy Pines Campground for a tour of the new "glamping" sites. These are camping sites set with luxury tents and many amenities you usually see in photos of luxury African safaris. I had volunteered to lead tours that morning and was told we had a special guest coming. Mrs. Bush arrived with a small entourage of Secret Service, family members and friends. The group gathered under the trees while the Secret Service agents quietly assessed the bumpy, wooded paths trying to figure out how Mrs. Bush would navigate it on her scooter. Before they could come up with a plan, Mrs. Bush announced, "Get out of my way boys, I'm coming through!" and scooted right past them without hesitation. Now that's what you call a woman on a mission – full of the spunk and spirit America loved!

– Lisa Linehan

Our favorite memory of Barbara Bush took place at the Nonantum Resort in Kennebunkport during a function for Southern Maine Medical Center, the area's largest hospital. George and Barbara were scheduled to make a brief appearance at the beginning of the function and then leave for another commitment. Our band, *Straight Lace*, was performing when they arrived. Dinner was to be served during the event, but they were not scheduled to stay for the meal. It became obvious that Barbara was having a wonderful time listening to the music and feeling the energy of a "packed house," so when George announced it was time to leave, Barbara was adamant that they stay to enjoy the band, dinner and a very festive evening. Because they were not expected to stay for dinner, and the room was absolutely full, they ended up dining with us at the band table. What an honor to have played a role in the changing of their original plan.

– **Fuzzy & Helen Farnsworth and Straight Lace**

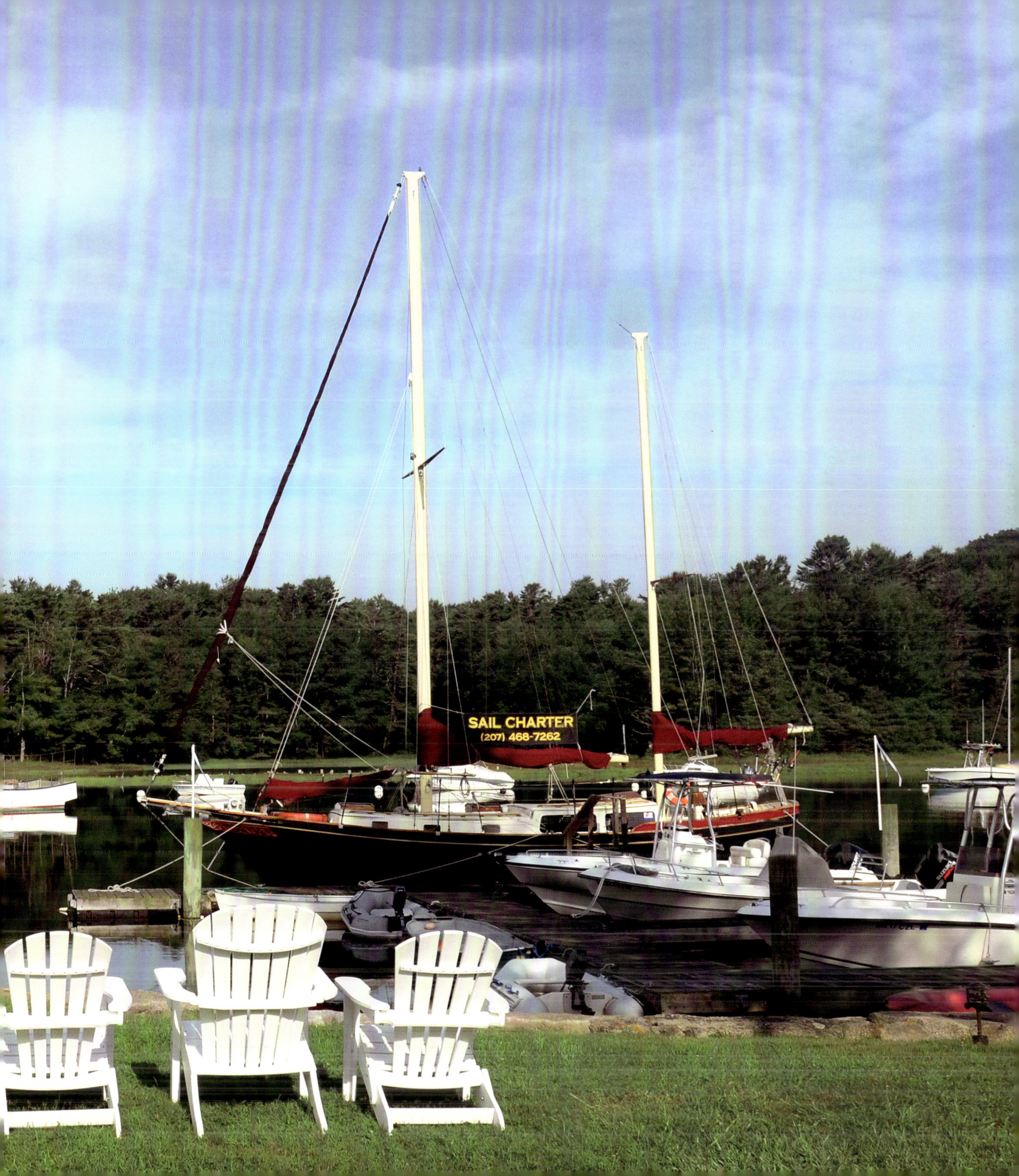
SAIL CHARTER
(207) 468-7262

Mrs. Barbara Bush. I have never known another person like her. She handled life, fame, politics, family, tragedy and love as an example for all of us to live by.

I thought she was the toughest lady I've ever known. But what she taught me is that love is the most important thing. Love. Everything else falls in second place.

I've been on vacation with her, to her two homes, and always felt very comfortable.

I have to admit I was afraid of her at first. But fear turned quickly into respect and I kept my ears and eyes open, ready to learn from the master.

On a cruise in 2003 to Greece, I learned that sitting by your partner at a meal was not a good idea. She said, "If you sit by your partner at a dinner or lunch, or when you're driving home, what do you have to talk about? What can you share to your partner that you've learned?" At a dinner or lunch, she would have someone cut a deck of cards in two. Cut one card diagonally. One half would be drawn out of a bowl when you walked into the dining room. The other was on a plate. You matched your half and had a seat. So smart. It forced you to meet new people and learn about their lives. She was so smart.

I've seen her swim from shore to the ship we were traveling on with two Navy Seals. I also doubted my decision to get into President Bush's speedboat with him driving. When I asked Mrs. Bush if she was going with us she said, "Ha. No."

One time we went to their home in Houston. President Bush asked if we wanted to see their new hydro-swimming pool? Of course, we said yes! He said the best view is from their bathroom window. So Narvel, President Bush and I walked upstairs. Mrs. Bush, never looking up from her project, said, "Make the bed while you're up there."

I can't wait to get to heaven to hear Mrs. Bush and God talking. He gave her a wonderful full life. She gave us a lot to remember and live up to.

Mrs. Barbara Bush. Happy Trails to You, Till We Meet Again.

– Reba McEntire

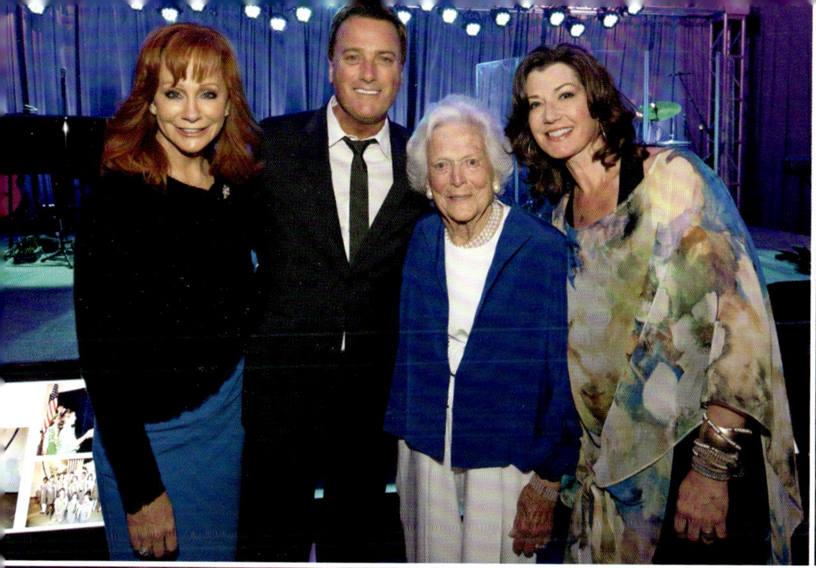
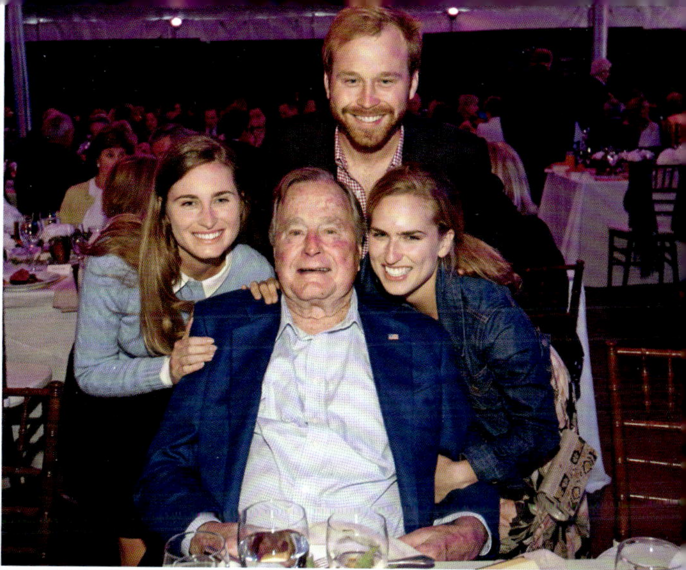
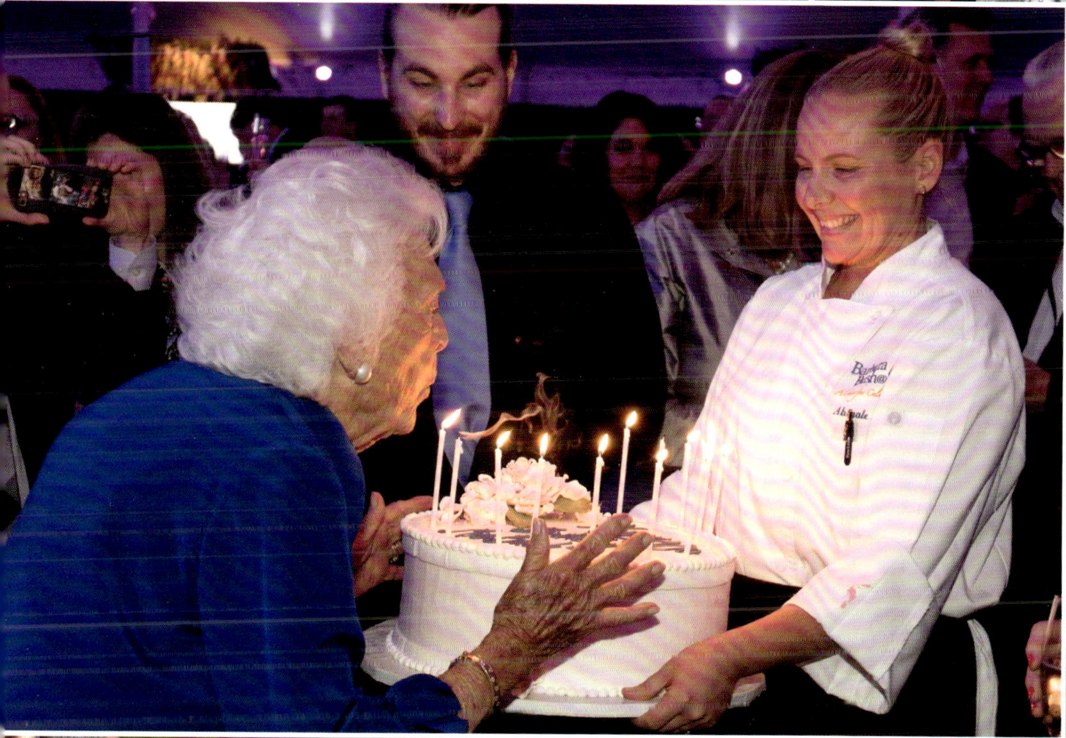
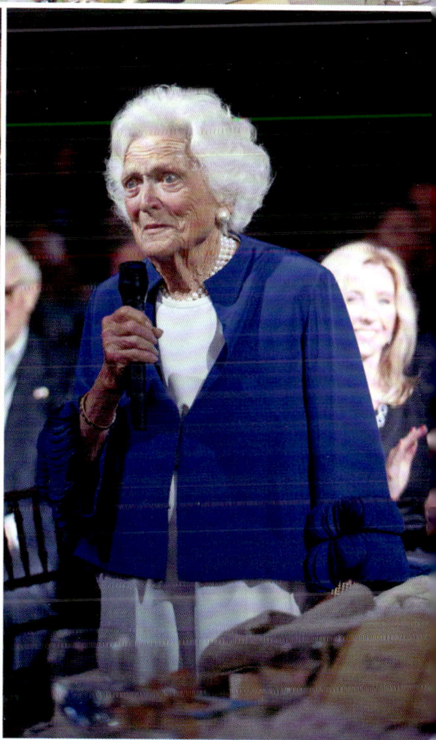
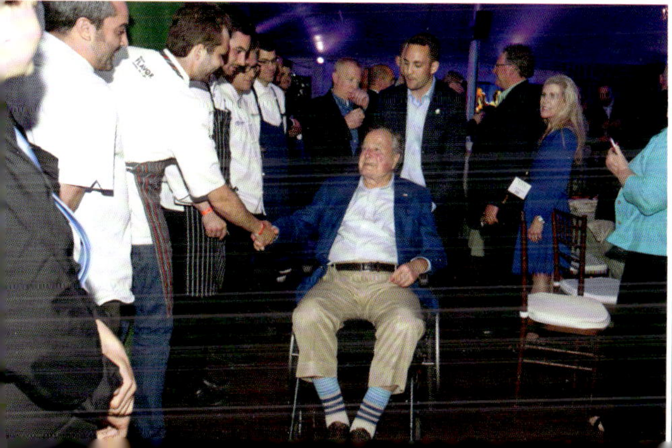
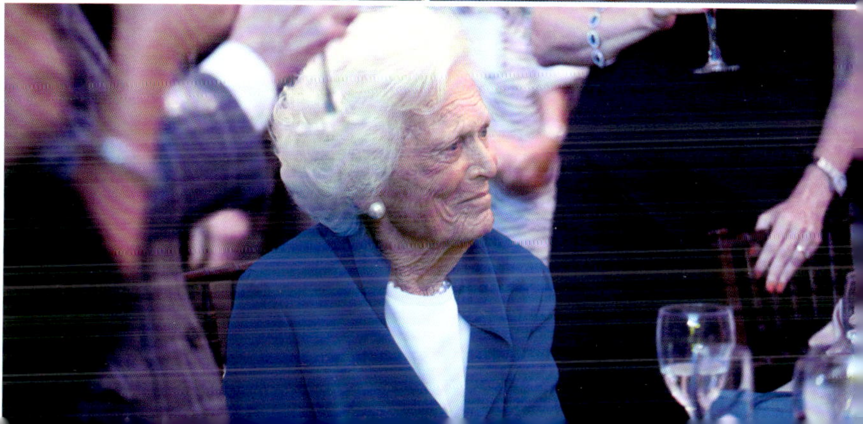

Every October, before President Bush and Barbara left to go back to Houston, we had a dinner together at Mabel's Lobster Claw in Kennebunkport. We took turns paying and Barbara and I always knew whose turn it was to pay! This was the year that President Bush told our waitress that he would take the check. Barbara said, "No, no, it's their turn to pay," to which President Bush replied, "If I had known that, I would have had two lobsters." I replied, "I'm glad you didn't!" and we laughed and laughed. P.S. Barbara and I split an order of mussels."

– Evelyn Paine

My wife Nancy and I were to host a fundraiser for our friend, Congressman David Emery. Our honored guests (and neighbors and friends) were George H.W. Bush, Vice President of the United States, and his wife Barbara.

The tent was up, the flag was flying, our lawn was mowed and we were ready! A big crowd had gathered as well as a sizeable group of press. We were advised to station the press off to the side to create a "bullpen" area. That seemed harsh so we declined. Big mistake.

As the official limo pulled into our driveway, Nancy and I moved forward to greet the Vice President and Mrs. Bush. Immediately the press mob pushed through everyone, preventing us from properly welcoming our honored guests. Barbara reached for Nancy's waist and held her close with a kind reassurance: "We'll be fine, just hold on." From that time forward, Nancy and Barbara were special friends.

– John Downing

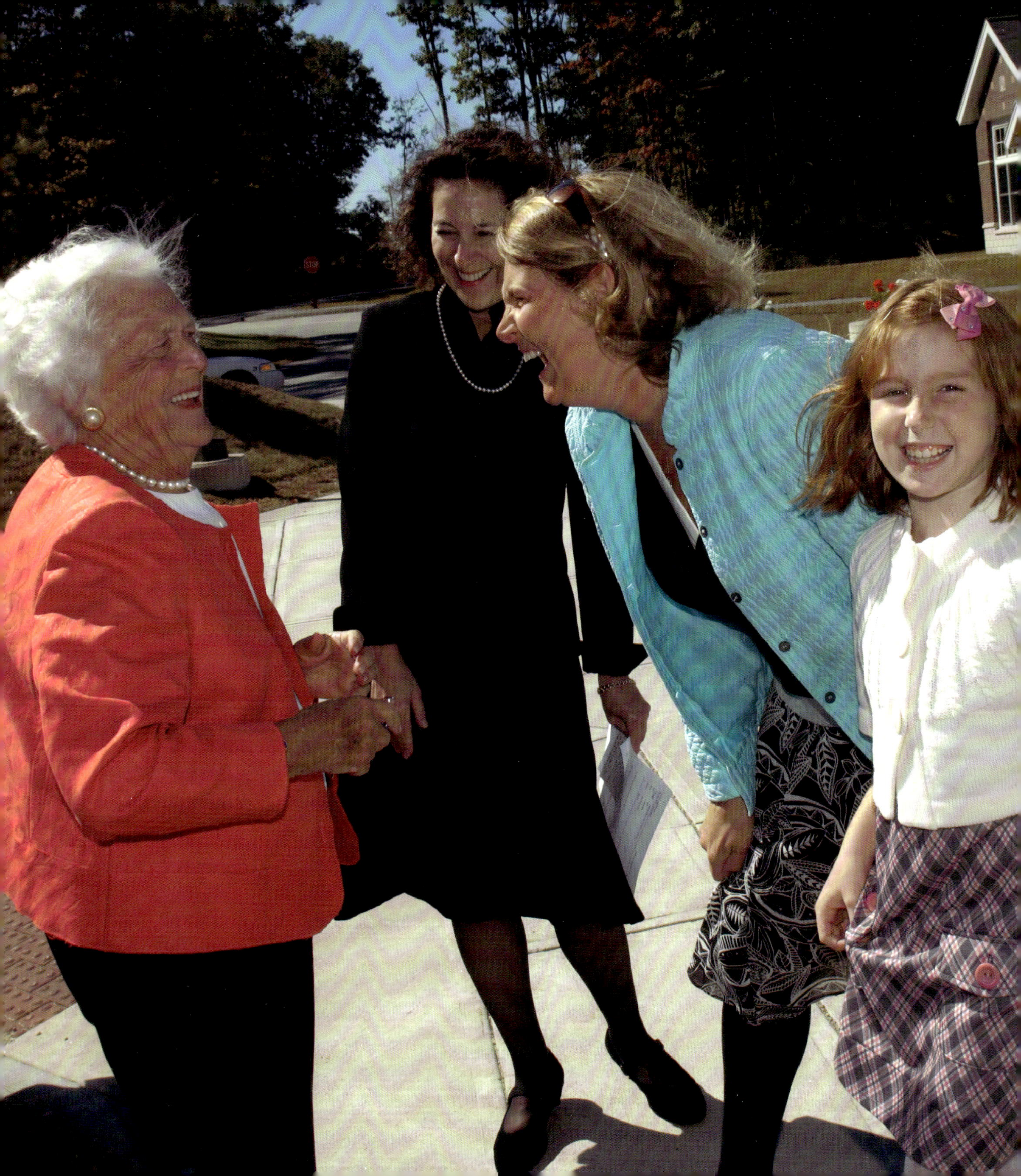
STOP

Mrs. Bush had a great sense of humor. The better she knew you, the more she would tease. When I grew a beard and went to Walker's Point to photograph an event, she told me my beard didn't look good and I should shave it. I knew she was joking, or at least I hope so.

Another time, we were invited to take a swim at the pool at Walker's Point and I jumped off the diving board and did a cannonball, just like the children. Mrs. Bush told me it was the worst cannonball she had ever seen. "Plus," she added, "your shorts are too low."

On another occasion, Mrs. Bush went to the new elementary school to read to the children and I was asked to be on hand to take photos. My wife, Cyndi, had set this event up and our daughter, Chloe, was a student there. Both Cyndi and Chloe were asked to join the principal to greet Mrs. Bush at the curb. Of course, I was there with my camera. When Mrs. Bush stepped out of the car, she looked over at me at said, "Who is that ugly guy?" Chloe thought it was hilarious. The photo at left was taken moments after.

When she was leaving the school, she turned to Chloe and said, "Now I know what Chris would look like as a girl." I was hoping Chloe wouldn't add up the two comments. (Chloe, if you're reading this, you're beautiful!)

Her joking always made me feel special.
– Chris Smith

Our stories with President and Mrs. Bush are many like others I'm sure. One of our favorites is when Helen and I went to Houston and ended up having dinner with both Bar and 41. We had told Jean Becker, President Bush's chief of staff, that we were coming to Houston to see our friend, George Dvorsky at Theatre Under the Stars (TUTS), a renowned venue in Houston. Jean later contacted us and asked if we would mind if President and Mrs. Bush joined us. Mind? Hardly.

Halfway through the meal in Houston Bar asked us to switch places so we could share some time with each of them. It was so thoughtful and gracious and allowed us to share time equally with both of our hosts during the meal.

Later that evening we all went to TUTS to see our friend George in *Anything Goes*. George walked out on stage and waved in our direction. Bar turned to us and said, "Oh look! He waved to you!" like we were the important people. At intermission, we all went backstage. Bar held George's dog for a photo op and said, "He is very heavy." It was a Pomeranian.

The trip was such a treat for us, the first of several such trips to see them over the years. What a wonderful memory!

— Bonnie Clement, Owner, H.B.Provisions

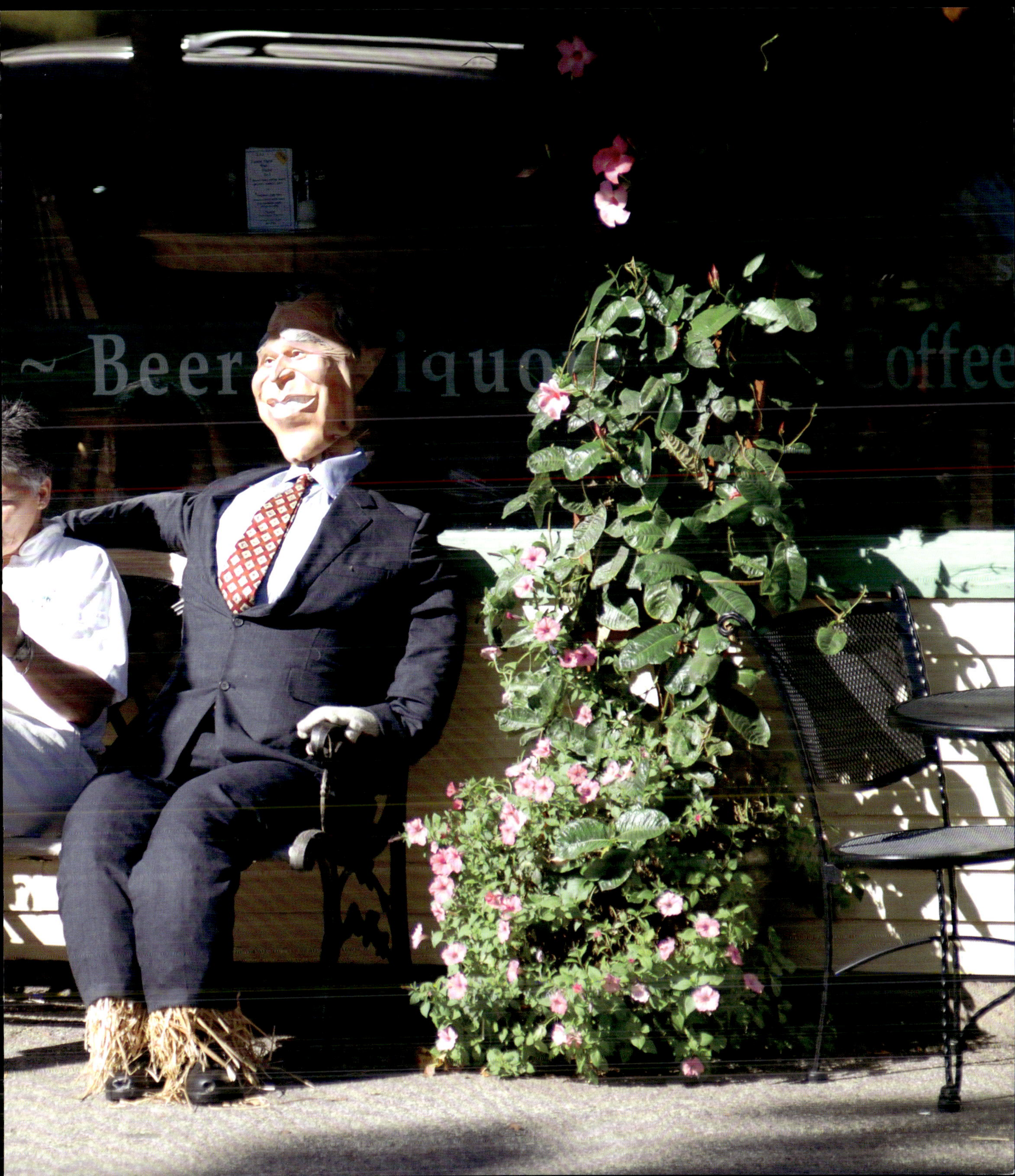
~ Beer

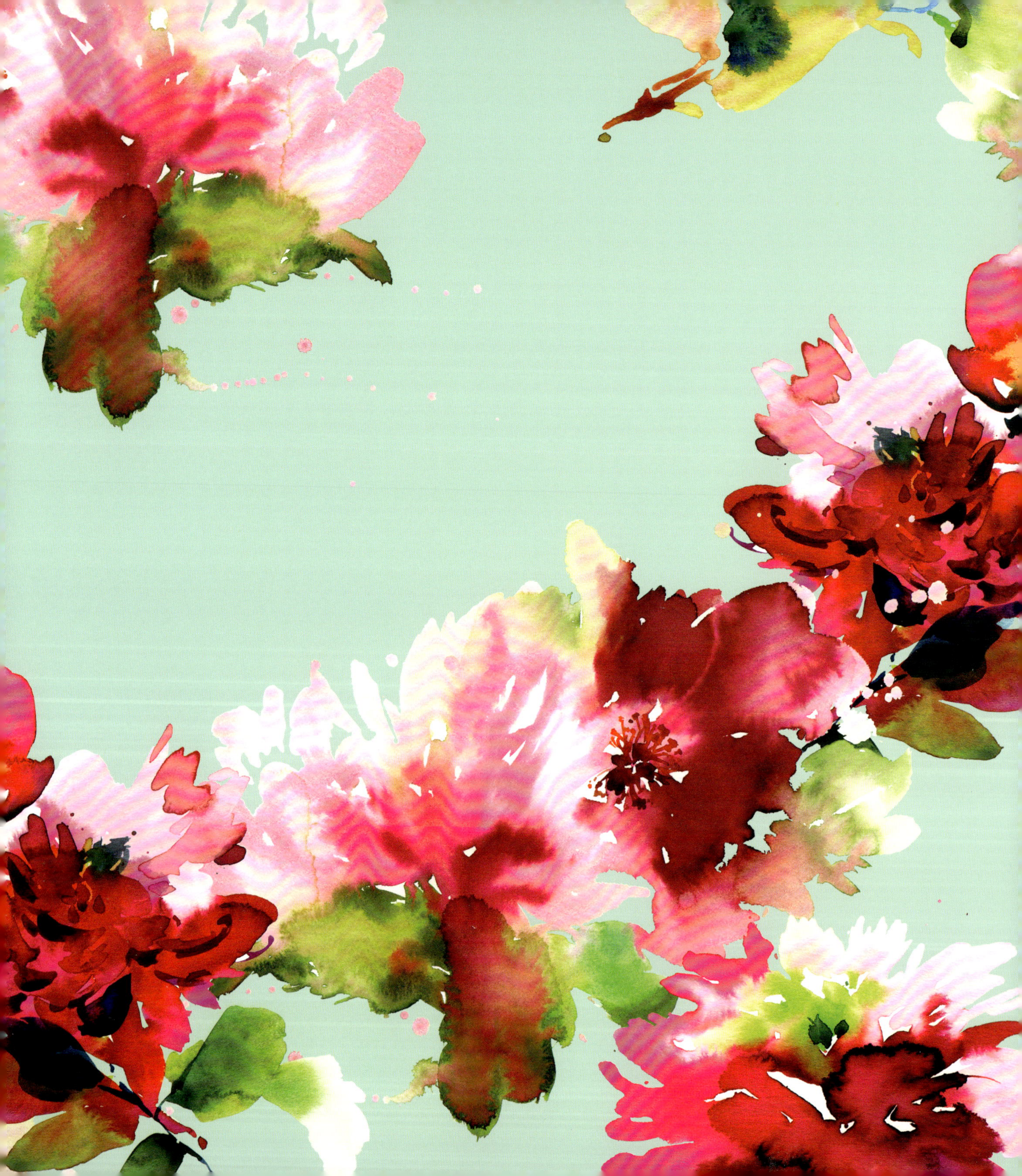

WALKING THE DOGS

✣

"Cherish your human connections: your
relationships with friends and family."

– **Barbara Bush**

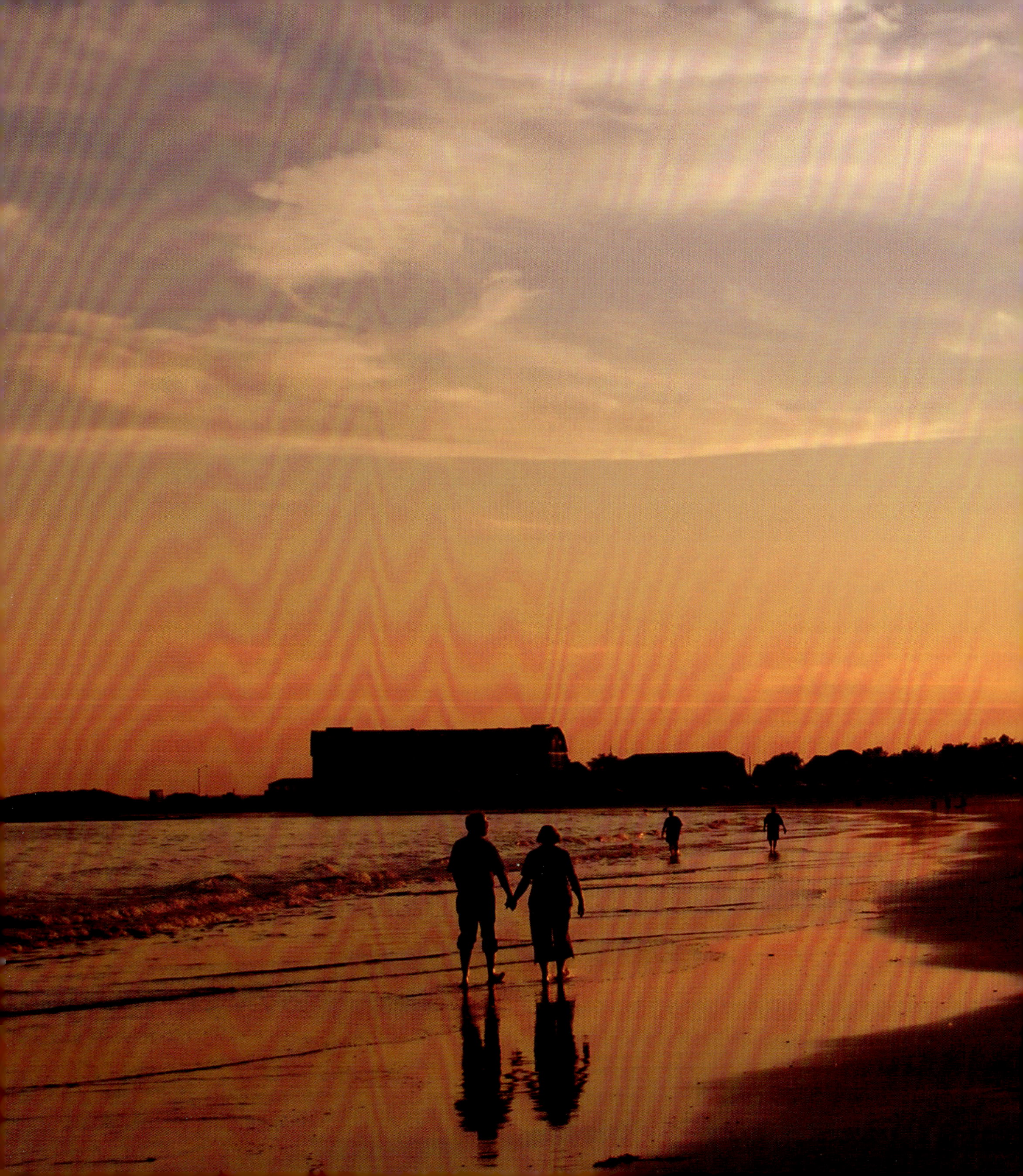

I first met Barbara Bush on Gooch's Beach seven years ago. I was walking my puppy *Rosie*, a miniature Australian Labradoodle. *Rosie*, who loves everyone and loves to greet everyone, ran right up to Barbara Bush to say hello. Of course, Barbara said what a cute dog — even as *Rosie* jumped on her. I was mortified, but Barbara casually brushed off her pant leg and began a conversation with me. This was the start of a wonderful beach walking and e-mailing friendship with the former First Lady!

– Sharon Bates

We had many meetings with Mrs. Bush while walking on Gooch's Beach with our dogs. But one of the best stories comes from a time when my husband and I were seated behind the Bushes at an outdoor service at St. Ann's Church. My husband leaned over and commented to Mrs. Bush, "Barbara your hair looks lovely today." Barbara remarked in her usual humorous way. She turned to him and said, "Only you know which side of the bed I slept on."

– Carol and John Dromgoole

One day Barbara came into the gallery to meet our new dachshund puppies. In the photo I am holding *Heidi* and Barbara is holding *Greta*. Lucky dogs! Barbara said, "Well, you finally got it right with these two. That *Jewlie*, your first dachshund, was a spoiled brat!" She was right. *Jewlie* would not let Barbara pick her up. *Jewlie* also snapped at *Millie*, Barbara's famous pet.

— Evelyn Paine

It was always great seeing Barbara on the beach with "her girls" in the morning, whom she always lovingly referred to as being "naughty." She often came over to check out how our son Tyler's walker matched up with hers. She was always just so kind and sweet when connecting with children.

— Nate Snow

Barbara Bush was truly a unique personality — she entertained many heads of state and famous people but was also very down-to-earth and loved meeting and greeting the locals when she walked on Gooch's Beach. During her off seasons in Houston, Barbara was always interested in hearing from me — asking about *Rosie* and my husband Glen and commenting on photos of the beach that I frequently e-mailed her. Barbara Bush touched many lives in the Kennebunks and she will be missed very much by the community.

— Sharon Bates

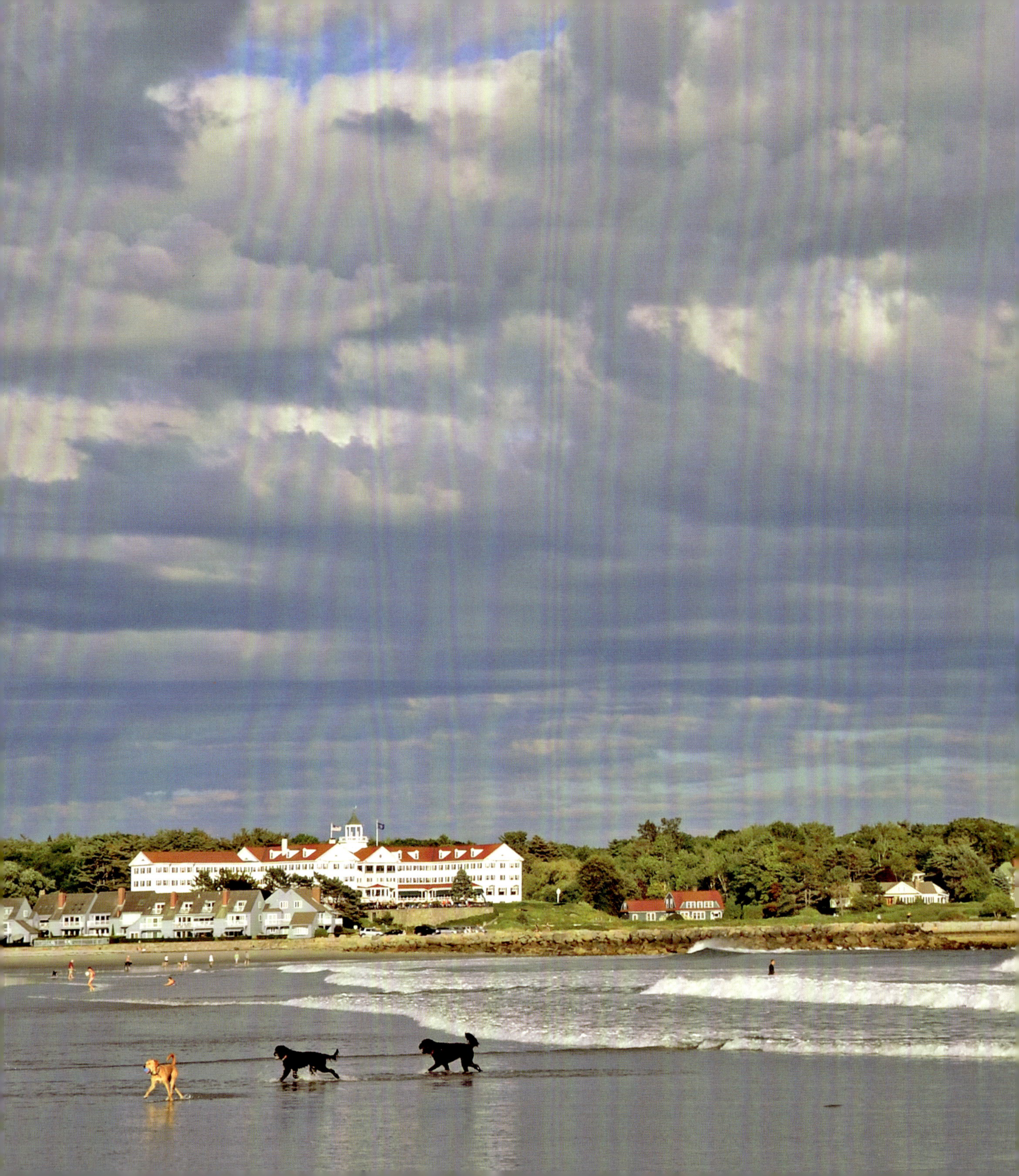

Late one afternoon in June 2012 on a dreary, rainy day, I decided to take my pug puppy, *Happy*, out for a walk. *Happy*, a spoiled southern California girl who had never seen rain, did not seem overjoyed with the plan. I had to tug on the leash to get *Happy* moving but we eventually got out of the driveway, reached the end of our street, took a left on Boothby Road and before we knew it, had reached the beach. Usually there were lots of dogs for *Happy* to romp with but not on this day. We had the beach to ourselves, or so I thought, until out of nowhere *Bibi* and *Mini*, Mrs. Bush's pets, suddenly appeared. While *Happy* was thrilled to see and sniff them, I was absolutely shocked to see Barbara Bush. I had seen her on the beach many times before and had even walked with her occasionally but never thought she would be out on such a nasty day. She looked at me as if I had two heads and quipped, "Don't you know it's raining out?" She was always so quick witted and never missed a beat. After the dogs played for several minutes she said, "I am worried about you and *Happy* walking home in this rain." I said we would be fine but she wouldn't hear of it. Next thing I knew, Bar, *Bibi*, *Mini*, *Happy* and I all piled into the back seat of the Secret Service car for the short ride home. Just when I thought *Happy* could not be any more spoiled, Bar pulled out a bag of treats and gave her the first one since she was a guest. *Happy* was very happy.

– Nancy Sosa

A couple of summers ago, I put on my favorite well-worn and faded gardening jeans. Although they sported holes in the knees and looked unkempt, I wasn't worried because I had planned to do yard work on that beautiful, warm, sunny day.

About half way through the morning, I realized that I needed a few things at the grocery store. Before going, I figured I'd check with my husband to see if he needed anything. As I approached him in the garage, telling him of my plans, he looked at me and said, "You're not going out in public in those pants, are you?" Why? Who cares?" I responded. "I'm not gonna see anyone. I just have to go and get a few things. I'll be right back." Off I went.

Later that afternoon, my husband suggested that we take our dog, *Wuggy*, a Poodle Llhasa mix, to the beach. What a great idea! I could take a break from yard work.

As I walked towards our truck, my husband looked at me and said, "You're not wearing those pants, are you?" "Yes, I am," I responded, "C'mon who's gonna see me?" Off we went.

Initially when we got to Gooch's Beach, *Wuggy* had his leash on. Seeing that the beach wasn't that busy, once we got to the sand I decided to unleash him. As I raised my head from being bent over, I realized it was too late! *Wuggy* was racing full speed ahead, straight for the water — straight for two small dogs scampering about an elderly, white-haired woman who was being followed by a tall, unassuming young man, about 10 yards behind. Oh, my God! It was Barbara Bush! Oh, no ....*Wuggy*! Come back!

I quickly ran to untangle *Wuggy* and Mrs. Bush's two dogs, apologizing to no end, while trying to put him back on his leash. "Mrs. Bush, I'm so sorry that my dog charged at you and your dogs," I blurted in my embarrassment. "I shouldn't have let him off his leash."

Mrs. Bush gave me a reassuring look and replied, "It's all right." Then she glanced down at my pants. She smiled a warm, beautiful, half laughing smile.

"My dear, did you know you have big holes in your pants?" she asked. "Yes, they're my gardening jeans," I replied. I then proceeded to tell her about how my husband didn't want me to go out in public wearing them, because someone might see me! She laughed and responded, "My granddaughters pay big bucks for jeans like those!"

My husband was within earshot of her comment. All he could do was smirk. After all, who was gonna see me? I love my Barbara Bush jeans!
– Kathy Jacobsen

I remember how supportive Barbara Bush was in the publication of our *Gooch's Pooches* book.
We had the audacity to ask her if she could be at the beach at 8am on a certain day to participate in a group photo for the book. She not only showed up, she was the first one there. She later told us that she wondered if she had gotten the directions wrong as no one had yet arrived. Eventually, everyone showed up and the photo was taken. It not only appeared in our book; it was widely shown in the news following her passing.
– Bob Dennis

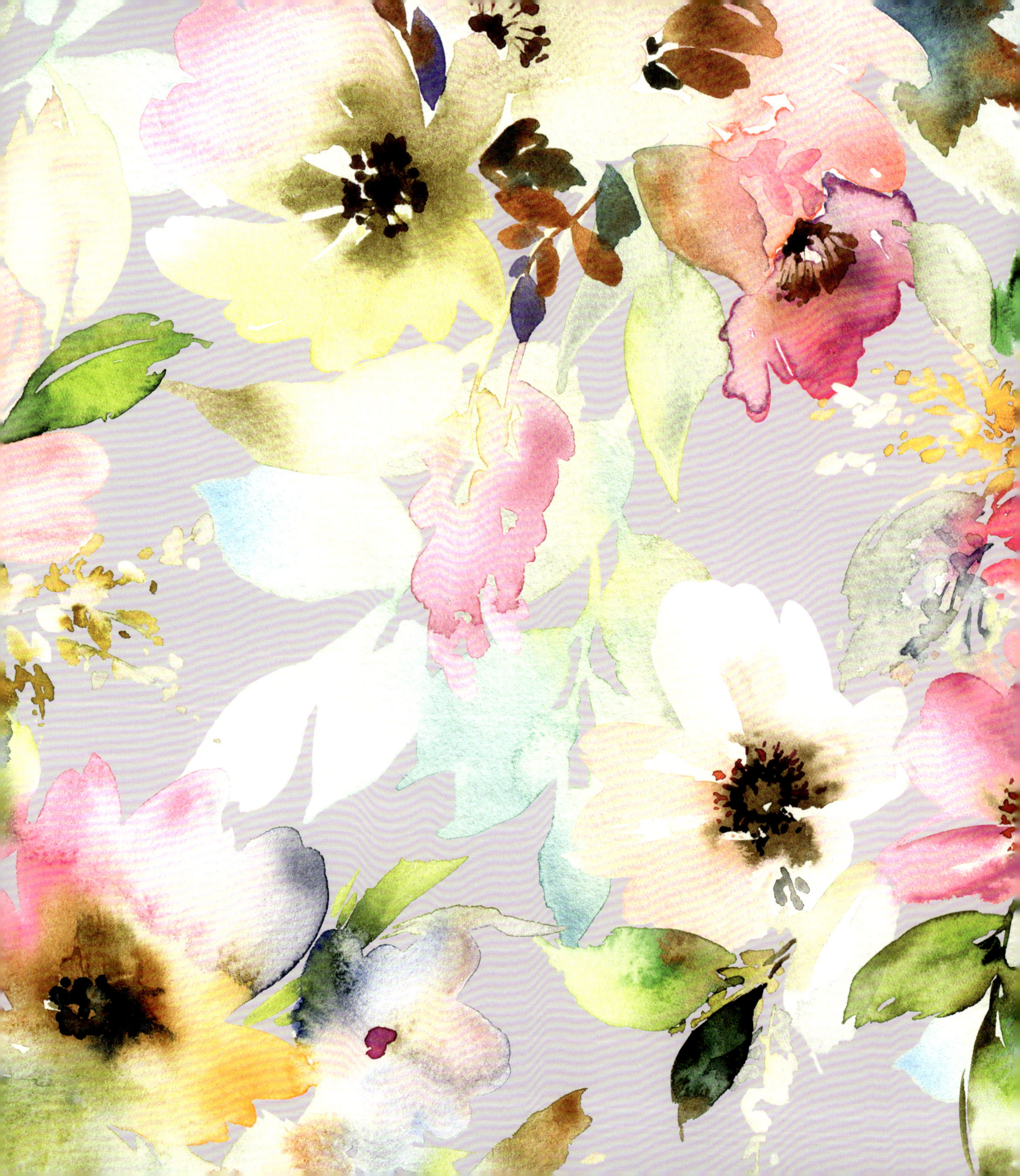

LIFE ON PARADE

✣

"Some people give time, some money, some
their skills and connections, some literally
give their life's blood.
But everyone has something to give."
— Barbara Bush

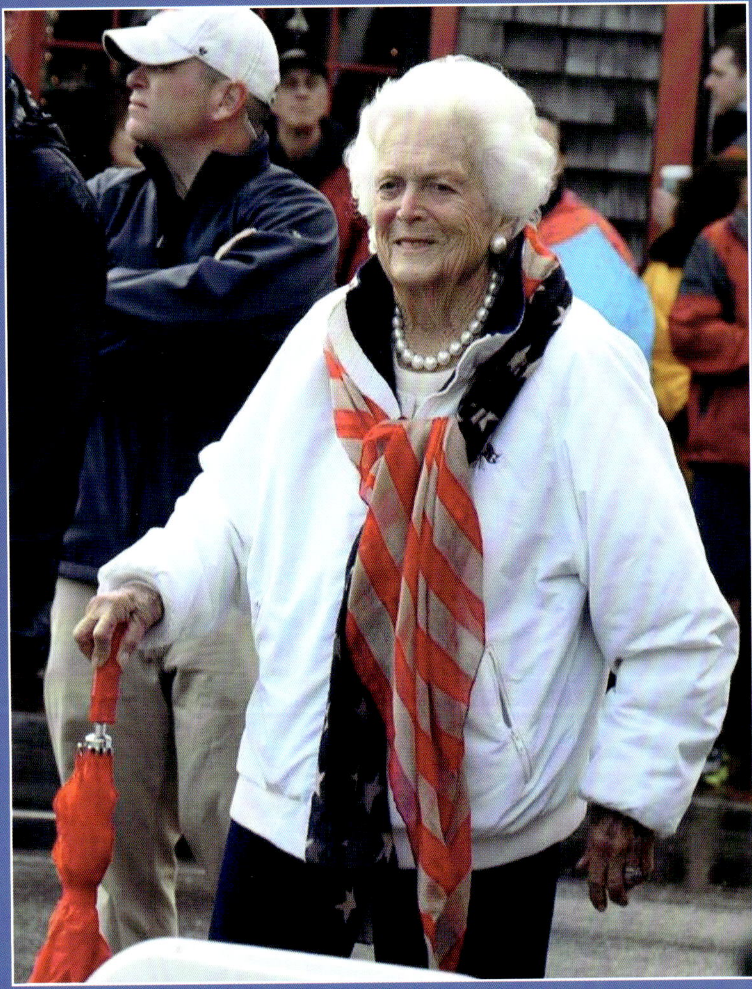

Dan and I have never personally met President and Mrs. Bush. But, we remember well the year that Tom Willey invited our daughter Elizabeth (Liz) McLaughlin and her husband, Chuck, to speak at Kennebunkport's Memorial Day parade. Both are Army Reserve officers. They came in their dress uniforms, met with the Bushes and sat with them behind the barrier in Dock Square prior to addressing the crowd. After Liz finished speaking, she returned to her seat next to Mrs. Bush. Mrs. Bush patted her on the knee and said, "You ought to take that on the road." It was an unsolicited gem that meant so much.

– **Sarah and Dan Beard**

As a Kennebunkport Memorial Day parade spectator one year, I complimented Mrs. Bush, telling her that "she was awesome." Then I added, "You're chic as well." She quickly shot back, "No, I'll stick with awesome."

– **Katie Pressly**

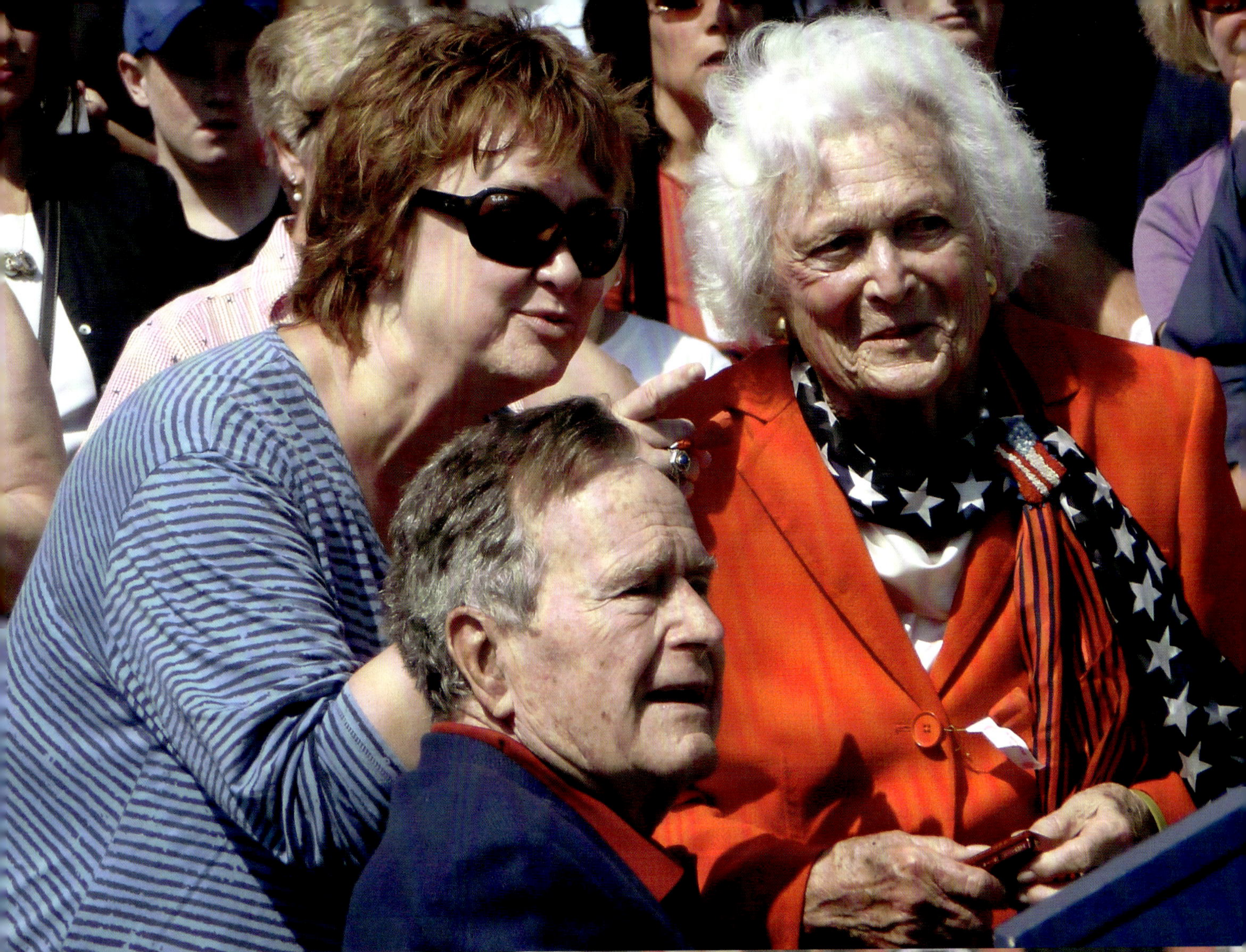

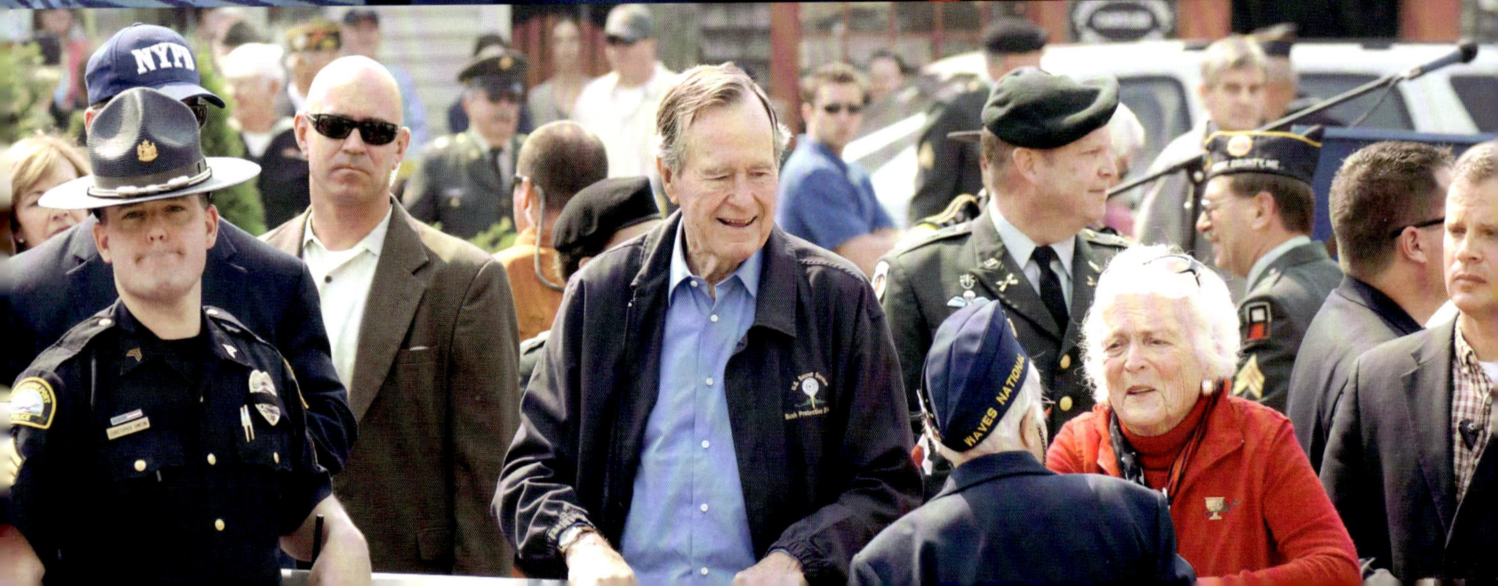
NYPD
WAVES NATIONAL

At the Kennebunkport Memorial Day parade a year or so ago, when Mrs. Bush required a walker to get around, I was standing in front of the Colonial Pharmacy, which was just to the side of where the Bush family was positioned behind a low temporary barricade, when I noticed an elderly woman waving a copy of Destiny and Power, the newest book on President Bush's life. She was obviously trying to catch the attention of the President or Mrs. Bush in the crush of humanity that often strained to get near them at the parade. I felt sorry for the woman as no one was allowing her near.

Suddenly I noticed Mrs. Bush slowly but deliberately shuffling with her walker toward the corner where the woman stood. Sure enough, Mrs. Bush had seen her and no amount of pavement was going to stand between her and the mission at hand. Slowly she moved toward the woman, step by slow step, until she had crossed about 20 feet of pavement. With a smile and a nod, she reached out and grabbed the book. Then she turned and repeated the route directly to her husband. With a clear gesture, she told the President to sign the book, which he promptly did. An agent or family member ran the book back to the woman, whose face lit up like she had just been given a million dollars.

Mrs. Bush didn't have to help get the book signed. She could have ignored the woman. Or she could have asked a family member in better physical condition to run over and grab the book. The fact that she didn't and went through so much effort to accommodate speaks volumes about her innate goodness and her recognition that such a small kindness would make a big difference in that woman's day.

– Tim Dietz

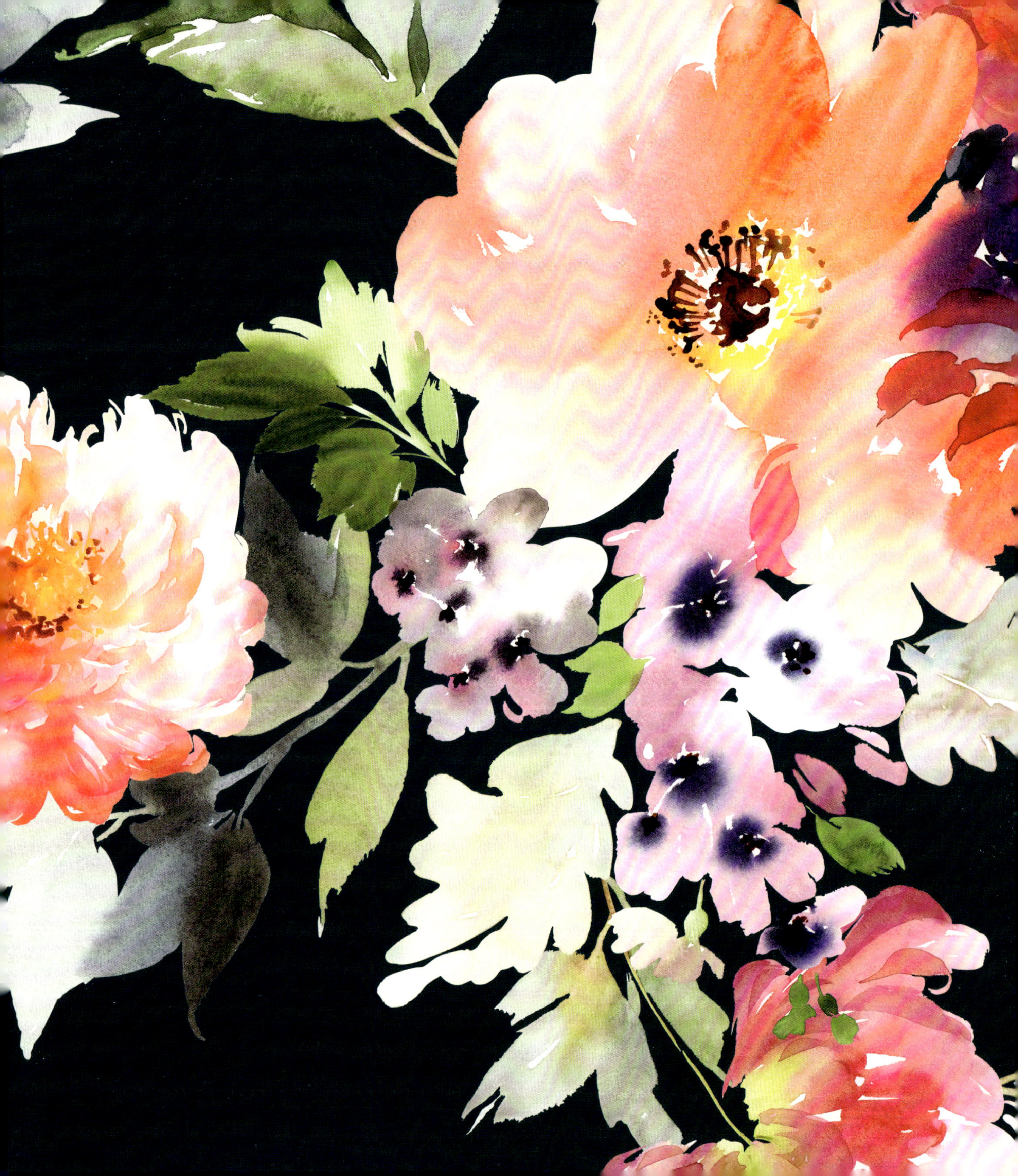

FOOD FOR THOUGHT

✣

"You must read to your children and you must hug
your children and you must love your children.
Your success as a family, our success as a society,
depends not on what happens in the White House,
but on what happens inside your house."
— **Barbara Bush**

In the summer of 2017 we were at an event at Vinegar Hill Music Theatre. We were outdoors at a preliminary dinner and I was sitting next to Barbara. She nudged me while looking up at the sky. She said that ever since her son George started painting she had become much more observant of colors. I will always be so appreciative of her comment, as I now notice colors.

– Bob and Dottie King

Several years ago at a large social function in Kennebunkport, as she passed by, I mentioned to Barbara that I hoped that she was writing another memoir. She emphatically replied, "No!" Among other things, I told her that I would miss her book recommendations. Then she moved on to speak with others. Later in the evening, as she and the President were leaving, she caught my eye and called out to me the names of two books, proof of her thoughtfulness and reluctance to disappoint.

– Linda Rice

Dottie and I were having dinner with the President and Barbara at Cape Arundel Inn. Dottie ordered a martini. The waitress came back a little later and asked if Dottie would like another martini. When the waitress walked away, Barbara said that a waitress should never ask if you want ANOTHER martini...she should ask if you want a martini.

At another time, on a September afternoon, we were having lunch at Walker's Point. Dottie was sitting next to President Bush and I asked him if he knew who the most famous Yale graduate was. He looked at me with a grin and then I answered...Eleazar Wheelock, the founder of Dartmouth College. I then followed up by singing...

"Eleazar Wheelock was a very pious man
He went into the wilderness to teach the In-di-an..."

Barbara got a big kick out of that tune.

– Bob and Dottie King
(Bob is a graduate of Dartmouth College)

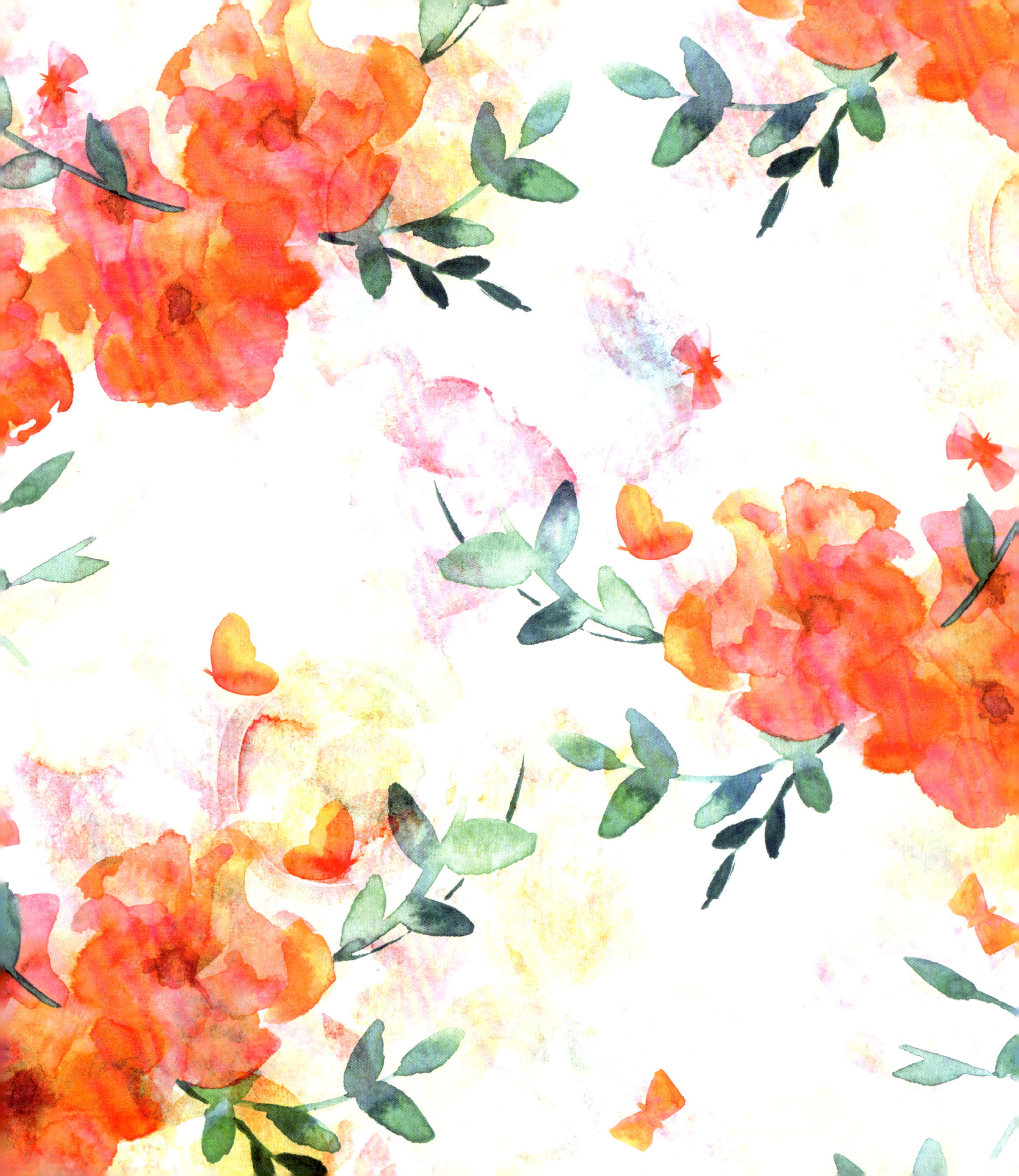

GROWING FRIENDS

✣

"As many of you know, getting involved in projects and causes can be very frustrating. There are days when all of us think to ourselves, 'What difference can I really make?'

A couple of years ago, when I was having one of those days, I decided to work in my garden in Maine. The instructions that came with the peonies I wanted to plant were very clear: Dig a deep bed, mulch, fertilize, plant flowers just so, and give plenty of water. They went on to say that if you followed the instructions exactly, the plants will not bloom the first year, but they will bloom the next and the next and every year thereafter for a hundred years.

Volunteer and philanthropic work is a lot like planting peonies — you may not see the results right away...but you ARE planting seeds that one day will sprout and bloom forever."

– **Barbara Bush**

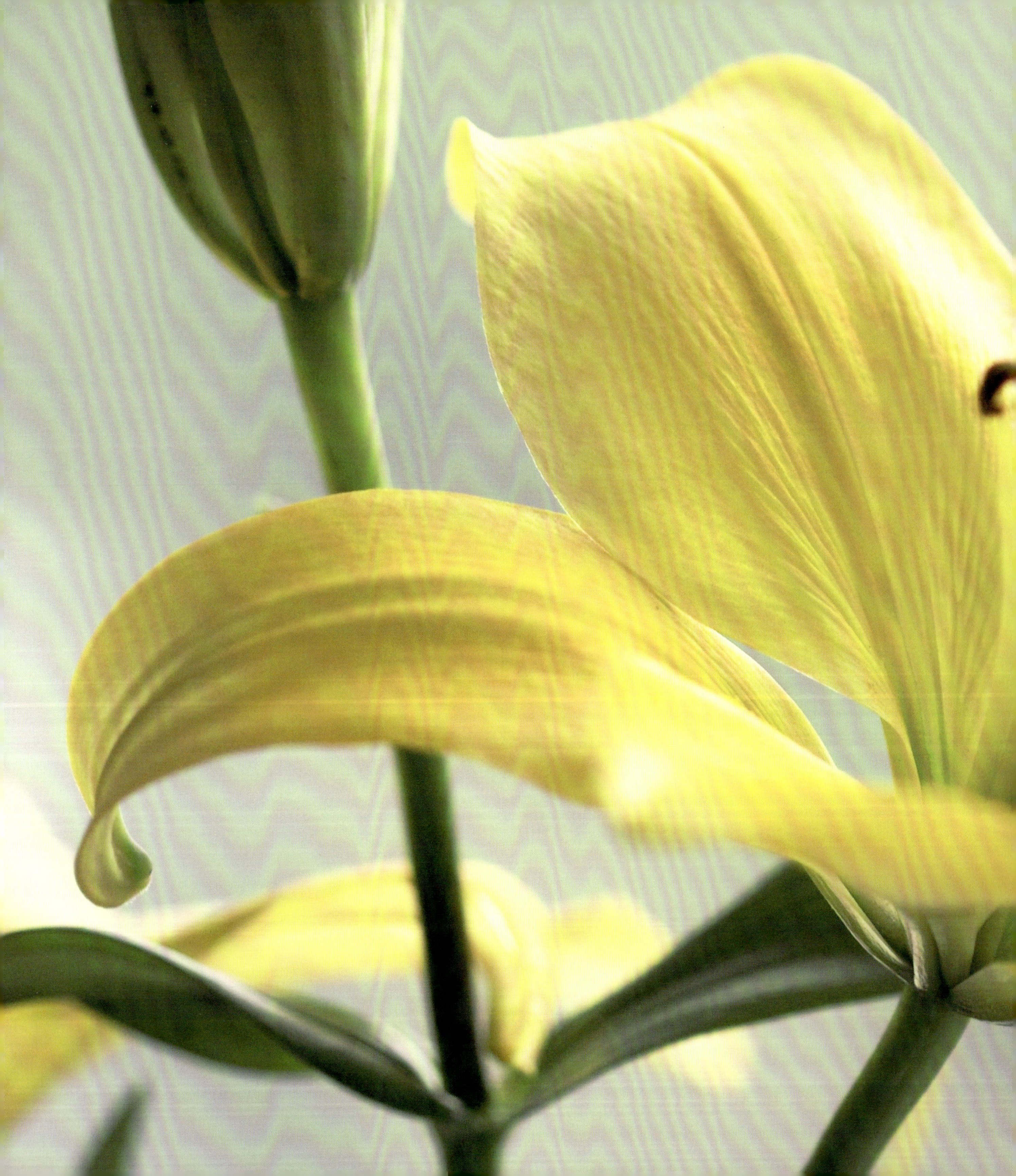

Many years ago when I was living at a condo on Ocean Avenue, I had the pleasure of a visit from Barbara Bush. When she arrived I was arranging flowers that I had just picked and did not notice pollen from the lilies had dusted my white blouse. To my embarrassment, Barbara noticed. "Get me scotch tape!" she said. I didn't know what to expect but I did as I was told. (We don't question Barbara!). She wrapped the tape around her fingers and gently lifted the pollen off, rotating the tape until I was completely clear of pollen. I just stood there in disbelief and said "Barbara, I don't believe what just happened." She brushed it off as nothing of importance and that was that! I not only learned a new trick for removing pollen but I became more aware of what a down-to-earth, warm and gracious lady Barbara Bush was. She was my friend and I will miss her greatly.

– **Jean Perkins**

It was September, 2011, and I was part of a large group of local people that was going to surprise Mrs. Bush with the dedication of Ganny's Garden, a beautiful garden space on the River Green near downtown Kennebunkport that was built by the Kennebunkport Conservation Trust in honor of Barbara Bush. At the appointed hour, Mrs. Bush was on her way home from a hair appointment in Kennebunkport. As carefully planned, as the Secret Service approached the River Green, they stopped and suggested to Mrs. Bush that she needed to get out of the car and enter the tent that had been erected there. I had been asked to give a short presentation and, needless to say, I was not accustomed to public speaking. It was not one of my strengths, but for Barbara Bush I would do anything. Mrs. Bush entered the tent and the surprise was awesome! I greeted and hugged my friend. Her first words were, "I'm not dressed well and I'm not even wearing my pearls!" That's how much of a surprise it was. As luck would have it, I was wearing a pearl necklace. I offered it to her and she was quite happy to borrow them. The event was precious. I survived my speaking engagement and Mrs. Bush (she insisted I call her Bar) was not only surprised but thrilled with Ganny's Garden. It was an honor to be part of this tribute to my dear friend, Barbara Bush!

– **Alicia Spenlinhauer**

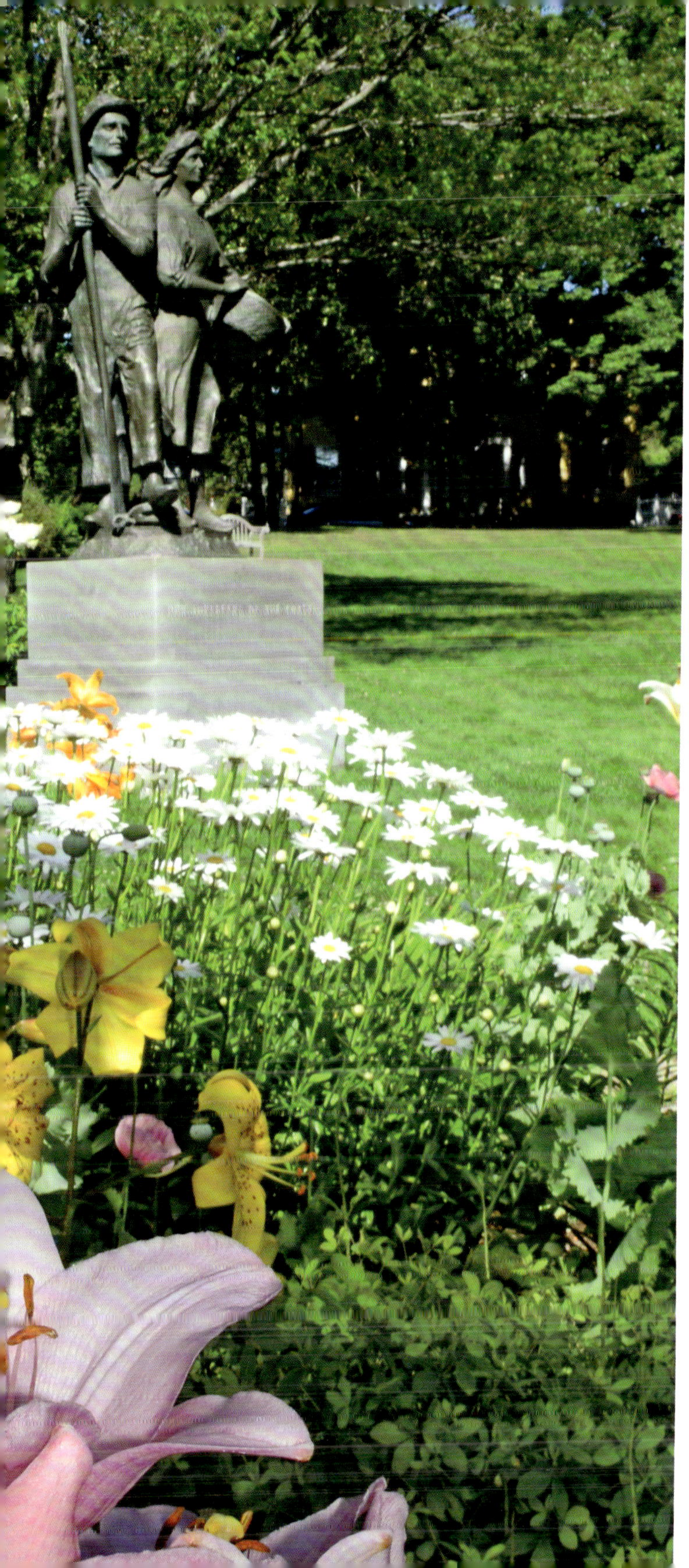

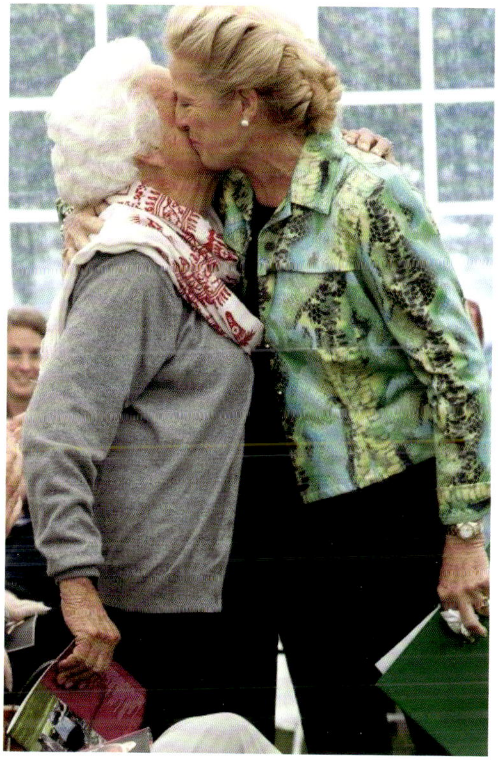

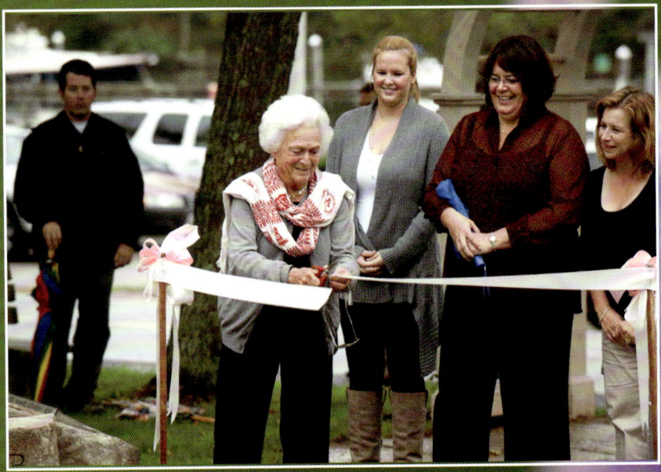
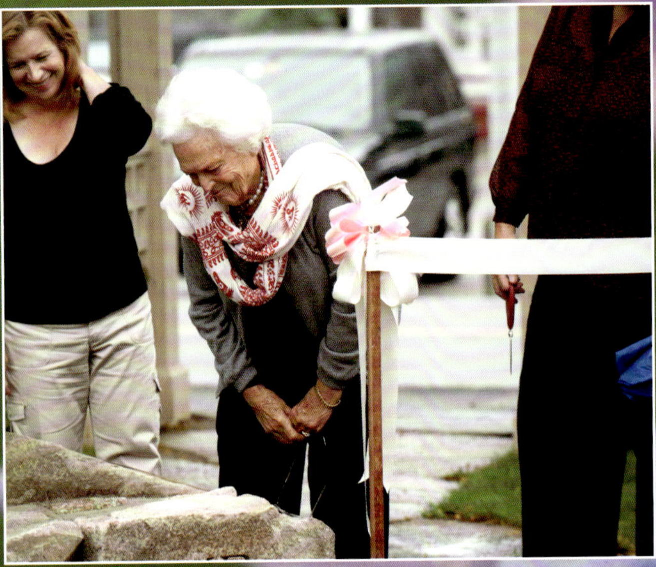
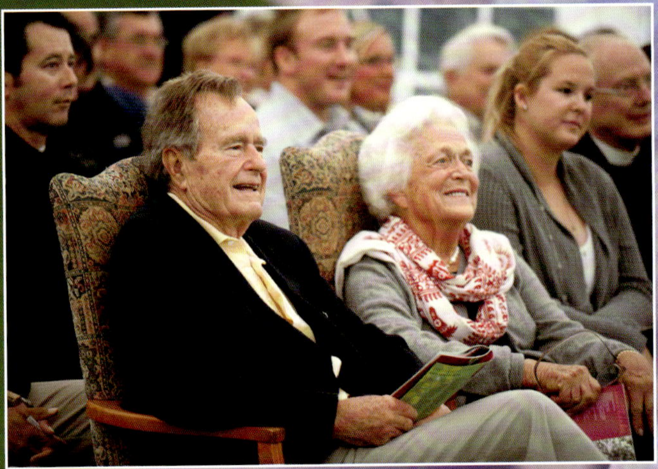

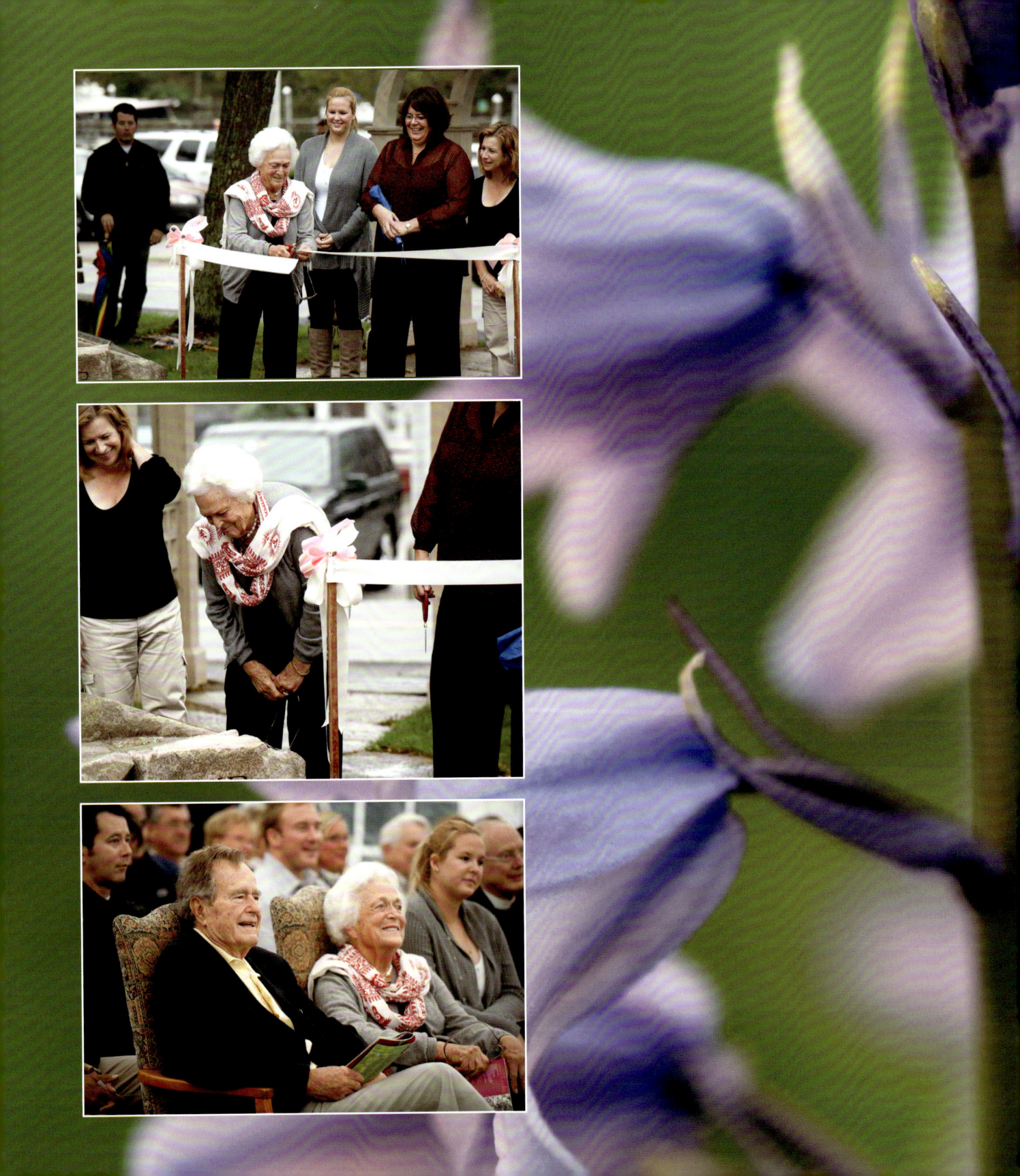

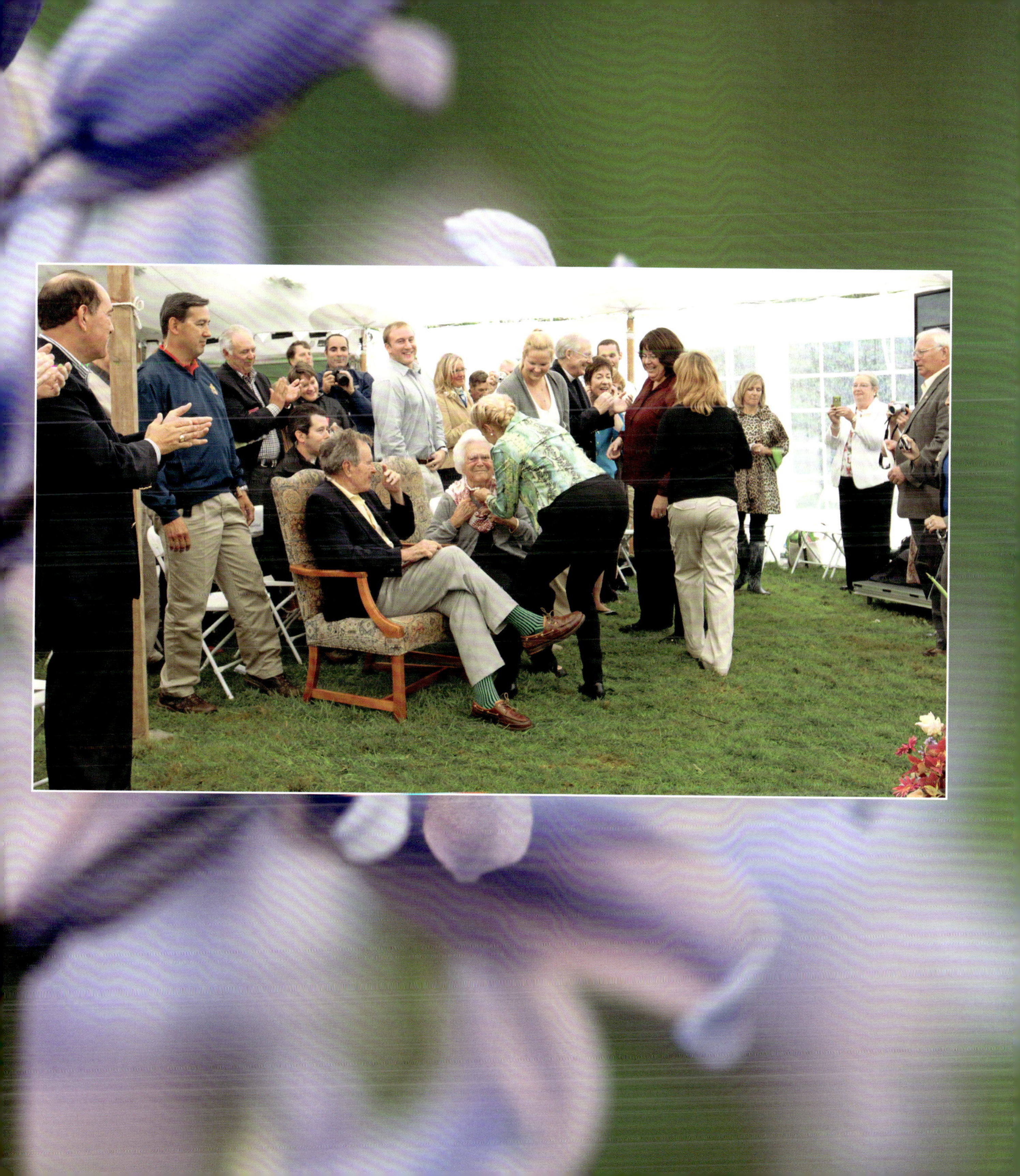

About 10 years ago, I moved to the U.S. and rented a house in Kennebunk. I came home one day and spotted the owner of the house, JoAnn Lapointe, and a gorgeous elderly woman down by the garden shed. Assuming it was JoAnn's mom I went down to introduce myself.

"Ingunn," said JoAnn, as if she was introducing the neighbor next door, "I would like you to meet Mrs. Bush!" I couldn't believe it!

It turns out that they had run into each other at the local hardware store and struck up a conversation about flowers. Mrs .Bush was in need of some type of support for her peonies and the hardware store didn't carry the metal peony rings that support the growing flower stalks. Overhearing the conversation, JoAnn said that Mrs. Bush was more than welcome to have her old peony rings. So the former First Lady of the United States heads home with a stranger to get what she needed to have her peonies at Walkers Point grow upright!

We chatted for quite a while. When it was time for her to leave a tiny little electrical car with a driver pulls up. I believe the car was a gift she received from her husband. She rolled her eyes and said, "This is just his green alibi for driving that monstrous boat of his!" and off she went.

– **Ingunn Milla Joergensen**

I was Mrs. Bush's Aide during the exciting White House years and the year following their return to Houston. I have very fond memories of working in the garden alongside Mrs. Bush.

I recall that a tulip was named after Mrs. Bush on a visit to the Netherlands and they shipped about 200 bulbs that Mrs. Bush and I planted around The Point one day. They were lovely and came up for a few years. My back does not forget the day.

One summer, we were all enthralled watching the progress of a sunflower that was enormous! It was not technically in the garden, but on the road leading up to the main house. It must have been 5-6 feet tall. And then one day, it was gone. We later found out that one of the nurses for Dorothy Walker Bush had cut it down and brought it "inside" for President Bush's mother to enjoy!

Mrs. Bush took great interest and pride in her garden and would show it off to visiting heads of state, dignitaries, etc. She would work in the garden every day. She was often seen covered in *Skin So Soft* with a beekeeper's hat and netting over her face and neck to protect her from the bees and mosquitoes because she was a magnet for them!

Peggy (Swift) White

In the early 1950's, I flew to Midland, Texas to stay with Bar and see her kids. She had a garden of daffodils coming up nicely along a fence in her backyard. The next morning, a mighty wind came up, and tumbleweeds were racing around the house, across the lawn, and slamming into the daffodils. "Oh Bar!," I exclaimed. "Don't worry," she replied, "that happens here."

In 1980, George and Bar bought Walker's Point and Bar became THE gardener. She turned the flower garden by the Big House into a superlative cutting garden; flowers abounded, inside as well as outside. Day lilies bloomed by the pool. She planted a lovely little garden by the steps of the President's office; here he would meet the Press for a quick announcement — the arrival of Mitterrand, the appointment of Clarence Thomas.

In October of 1991 the *Perfect Storm* hit Walker's Point; waves thirty feet high smashed over and into the Big House. Furniture floated out onto the rocks. Stones from the sea covered the entire front lawn. But, by next summer all was repaired and flowers bloomed everywhere. And so it has been with every storm thereafter.

No storm can get the better of a lady who can cope with tumbleweeds!
— Nancy Bush Ellis

The front walled-in garden at Mrs. Bush's is a cutting garden. This is no small feat. It's like gardening on a boat and Mrs. Bush wants no…and I mean NO…small flowers — only cutting flowers.

This rule is broken, however, when it comes to her beloved poppies. The pink Shirley poppies reseed in her garden every year and she very sternly warns every new gardener who works at Blackrock Farm that under no circumstances should they be weeded out.

This can present problems for the seasoned gardener who tries to give the other plants a chance to grow but we do our best and leave hundreds of poppies to flourish. I know they can be seen in a splash of pink from Ocean Avenue in July.

At the end of the year, we cut back the garden and although most of the cut back plants are left on the Point in a large compost heap, some of the cut back is taken to Blackrock Farm and piled on our own heap here at the Farm. This means that those poppy seeds have managed to find their way here to the Farm. We use the compost from our own heaps on our gardens and lo and behold — we have quite a few poppies ourselves.

When they begin to bloom at the Farm (as well as at the Point) people who shop here at Blackrock Farm walk by my big border toward the greenhouses and ask about the flowers. I tell them that they came from Mrs. Bush's garden and then give them a seed head or two for their own garden. There are descendents of those poppies all over the country, in fact, the world, tucked into pockets and spread across the gardens of people who are thrilled to have some of Mrs. Bush's poppies.

– **Helene Lewand,** *Blackrock Farm*

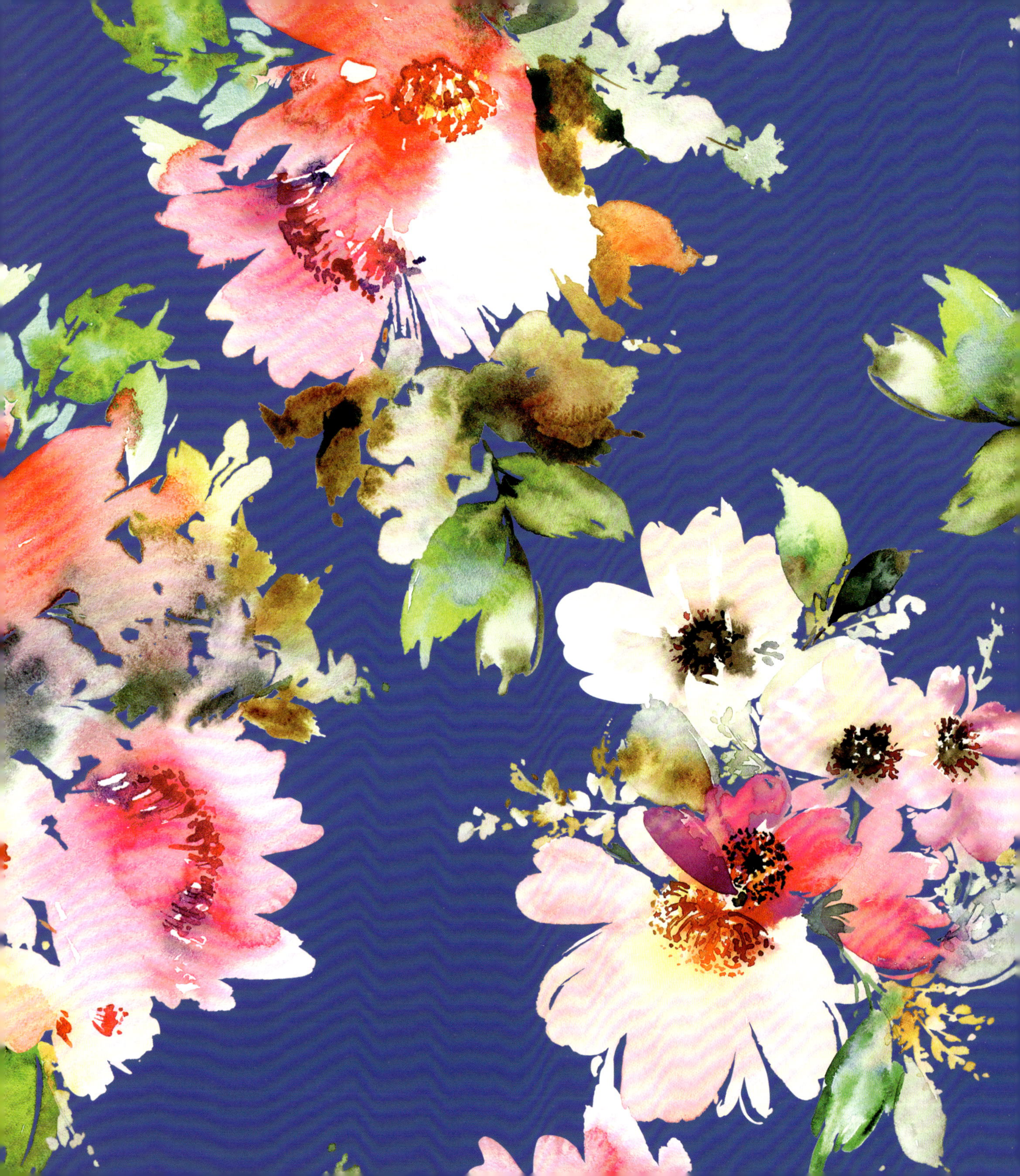

KEEPING THE FAITH

✣

"Never lose sight of the fact that the most important yardstick of your success will be how you treat other people — your family, friends, and coworkers, and even strangers you meet along the way."
– **Barbara Bush**

My family and I have lived in Kennebunkport for 20 years. We have enjoyed seeing the Bush family around town at Mabel's and Stripers restaurants as well as at their Sunday morning worship service at St. Ann's Episcopal Church in Kennebunkport.

On Sunday, June 21, 2009, we had our six-month old daughter, Alexandra Ann, baptized at St. Ann's. During the rehearsal for the baptism, we were advised that we were not allowed to take photographs during the ceremony. However, we learned that there was one person to whom a blind eye was turned when her camera was raised during each baptism: Barbara Bush. President and Mrs. Bush were regulars at the 8 o'clock church service, and Mrs. Bush, we learned later, had been taking photographs of children being baptized at St. Ann's for years. She would later have prints of the photos delivered to each family.

When we presented to the church for Alexandra's baptism, it was a very stormy day. Due to the storm, the baptism could not be performed at the outside Chapel, so we were inside the beautiful stone church. The ceremony went very well, and we stayed afterward to take some photos with the minister. It was then that Mrs. Bush approached us and told us that she had forgotten her camera that day. She asked if we would be at the church service the following Sunday so that she could take a picture of our newly baptized daughter. We said we would be there. Sure enough, the following week, Mrs. Bush sought us out after the ceremony — and she even cajoled her husband, the former President George H.W. Bush, into appearing in the photo with our family. Mrs. Bush was the photographer! It was a very special moment.

Later that week, an envelope with two 8 x 10 photographs of our family with the former President Bush — both of which were taken by Mrs. Bush — were delivered by hand to our home. Her kindness and thoughtfulness in remembering us will never be forgotten.

    – Liz and Dick Stockwell

Mrs. Bush was always kind and would make a point of coming out of church after the service to greet me. Some years ago, when I was courting Kiki, my future wife, Mrs. Bush apparently took note of the fact that it was a somewhat lengthy courtship. She was very fond of Kiki. After services she would walk out and say, "When are you going to marry that beautiful woman?" When we finally got engaged in the summer of 2012, Mrs. Bush was one of the first to come by with a congratulatory gift.

    – The Reverend Peter Cheney

We often saw Mrs. Bush discreetly snapping pictures during the 8am outdoor chapel service at St. Ann's. The subjects were usually babies and their families at baptisms. Many young parents told us later how surprised and honored they were when, on that Sunday afternoon, they heard a knock at the door and were given the signed photograph. Oftentimes, Mrs. Bush was sitting in the car and would take time to visit with those families. We were the recipients of one of these Barbara Bush photos. It was a picture of ML holding our four year-old granddaughter who had run up to hug her Paw Paw toward the end of the service. It was signed by both President and Mrs. Bush: "To Sydney — a picture of you with someone we love, in a place we love. Warmly, George Bush — Barbara Bush". What a treasure for our granddaughter (who is now 21)!

– Patty Agnew

On my first Sunday at St. Ann's Episcopal Church in Kennebunkport, Mrs. Bush pulled me aside before the service began and mentioned that she usually had grandchildren attending the service with her who would get "antsy" if they had to sit through a long sermon, and that she would appreciate my being thoughtful of that. As the brand new Chaplain of St. Ann's, I was a little nervous but after delivering my sermon, I looked down from the pulpit at Mrs. Bush and was relieved to see a "thumbs up" accompanied by her warm and gracious smile!!

– M.L. Agnew

For many years the Bushes attended the First Congregational Church in Kennebunkport, a small lovely historic church at the crossroads of Log Cabin Road and River Road. The first Sunday they came to church after winning the election President Bush got up and said, "WE want you all to know that we are still George and Barbara to you."
— Carolyn Broad (Maden)

A man walked into the office and asked if he could use the phone to make some "urgent" calls. After a (long) while, I suggested that he might wrap up his conversation, whereupon he told me that he would be back — in church. Then late that night, he left a strange and threatening voice mail. Needless to say, the next morning, we notified the Kennebunkport police, and they were responsive. But so too was Barbara Bush!

That next Sunday, I walked into the sanctuary and couldn't help but notice a bevy of tall, strong, (and handsome) young men. Unbeknownst to me, she had heard of our plight, and sent out some of her own Secret Service personnel — as extra re-enforcement. The man did, in fact, appear. But needless to say, I had no doubt that we were safe! Never will I forget her act of kindness.

The first time the President and Barbara Bush joined us in worship at The Church on the Cape, it was immediately apparent that they both truly loved church. By their attentive listening to Scripture, and their obvious joy listening to the music, it was apparent that they enjoyed the service. No dozing. It was clear that they knew why they were there. It was truly a wondrous gift to be able to worship together.

– Ruth Merriam (Rev.)
Pastor Emerita, Church on the Cape

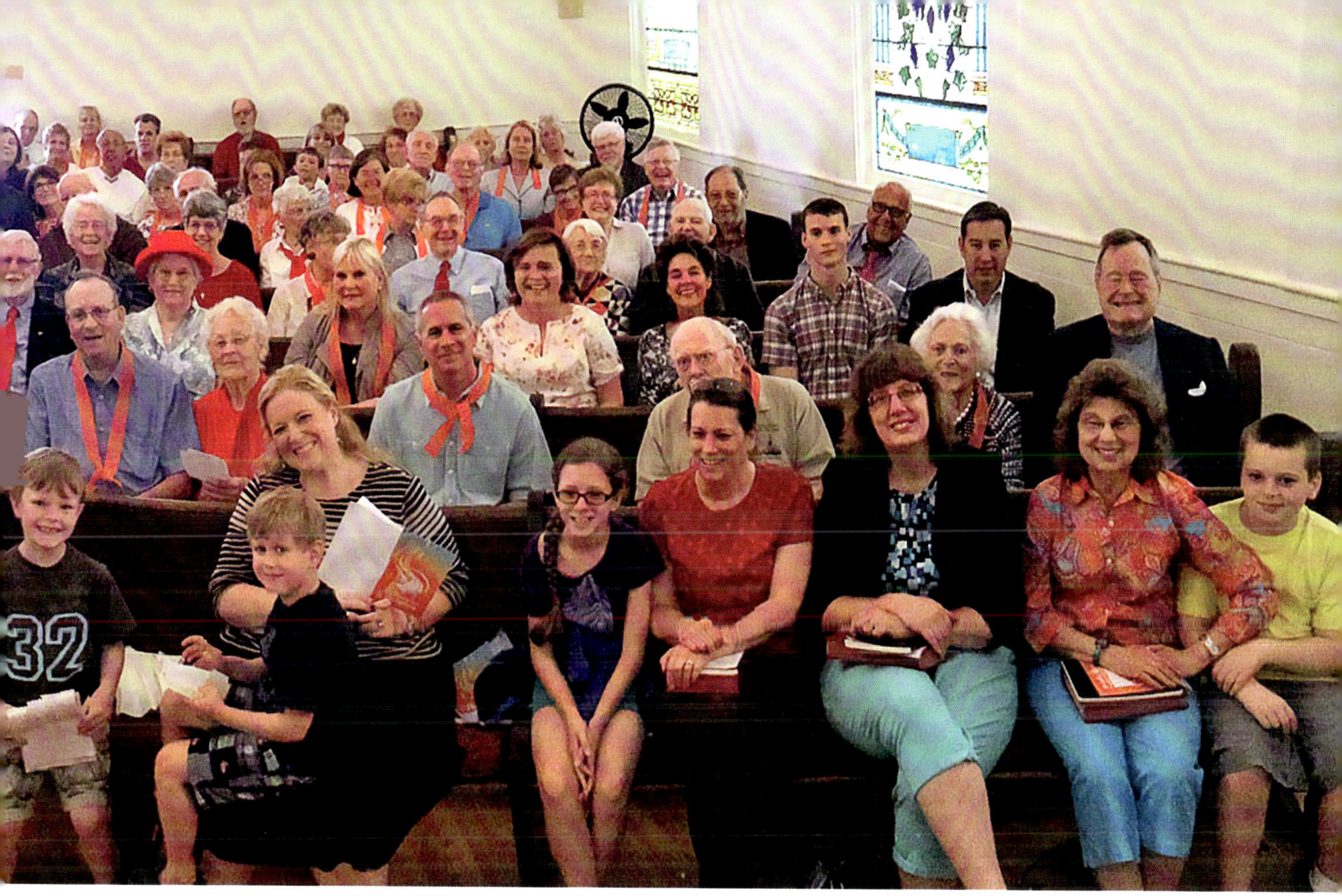

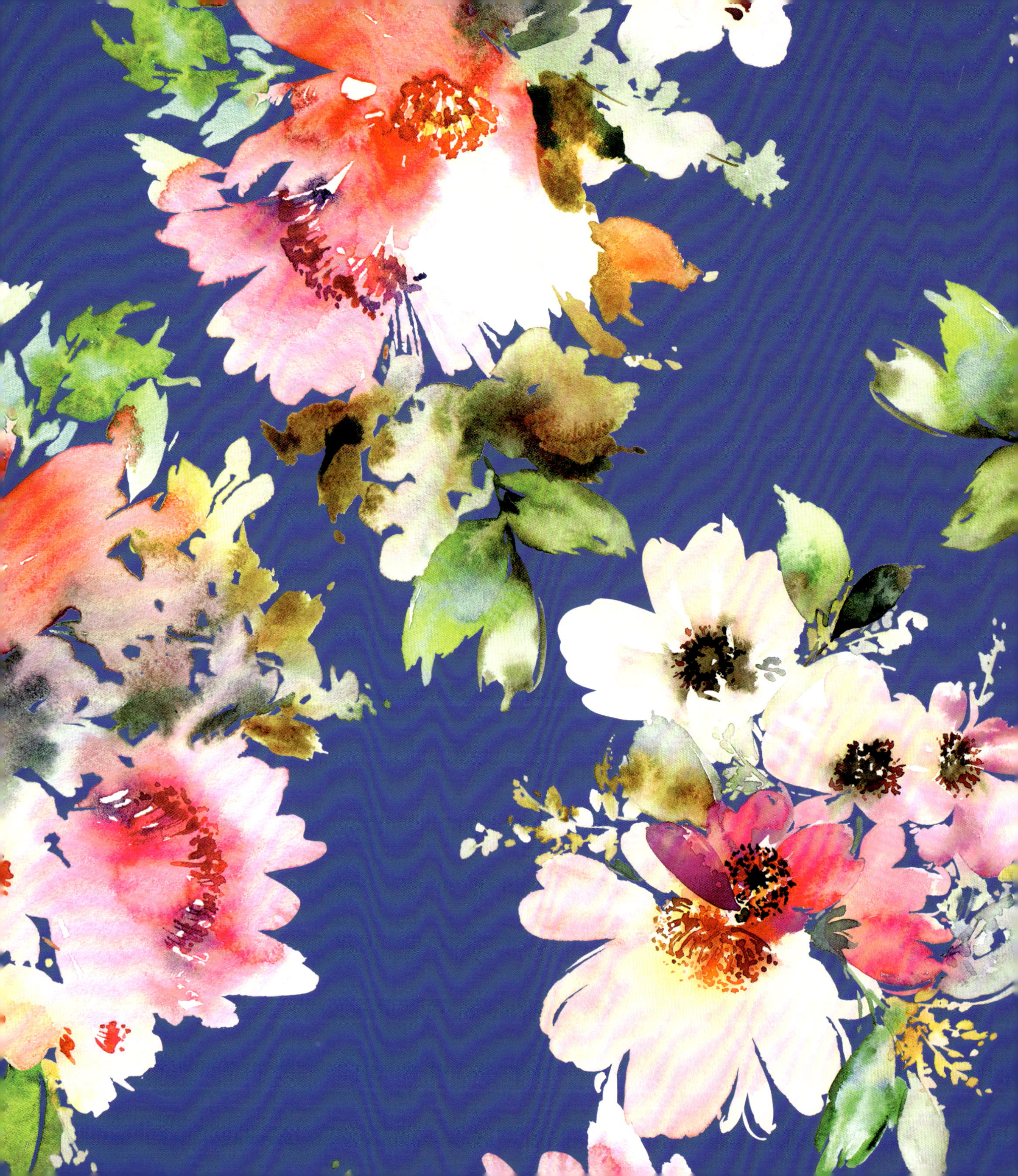

ON POINT

✣

"Why be afraid of what people will say? Those who care about you will say, 'Good luck!' and those who care only about themselves will never say anything worth listening to anyway."
– Barbara Bush

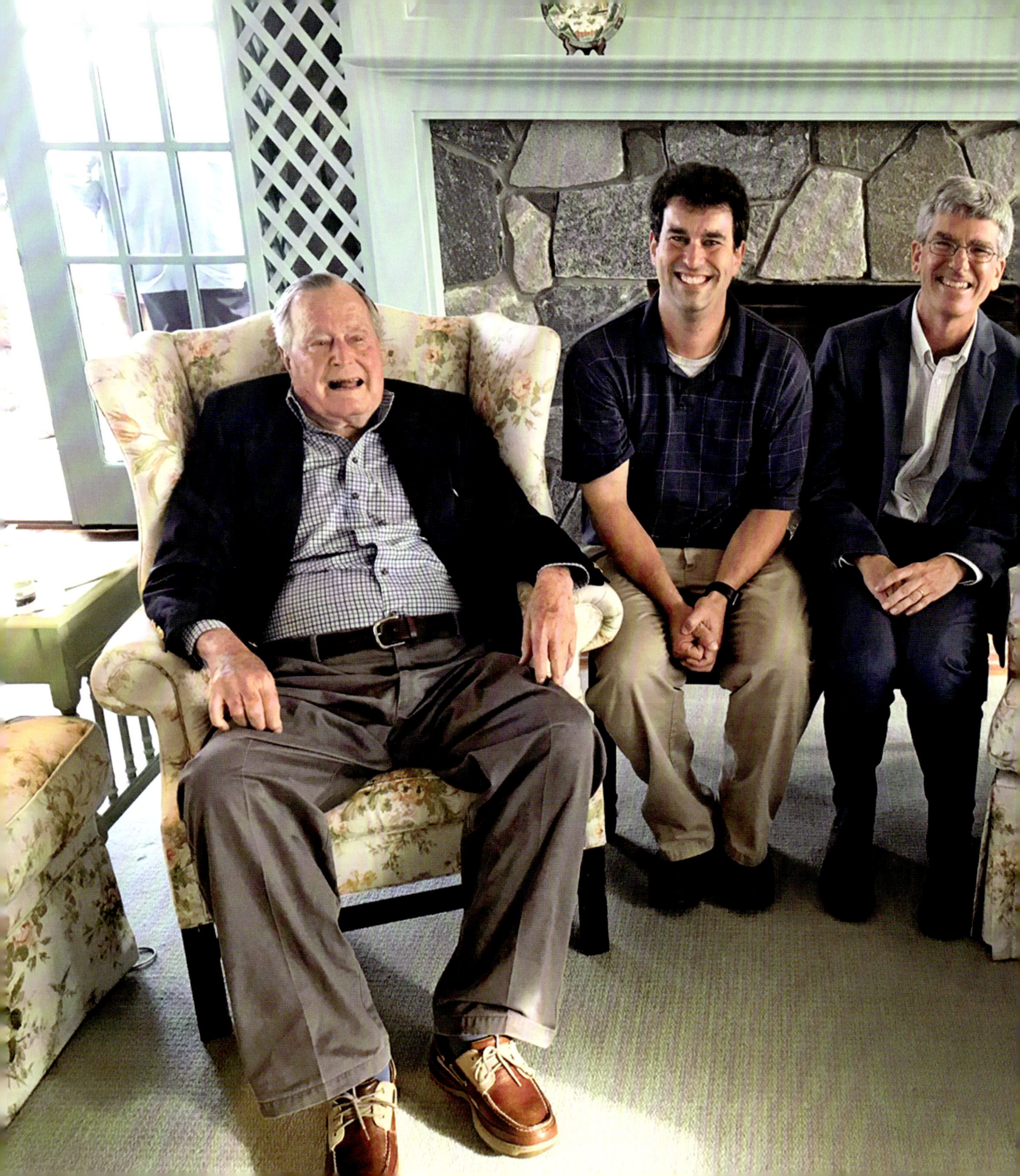

When I first started working for President and Mrs. Bush in the Spring of 2013 at their Walker's Point summer home, my shifts were often 24 hours long, several times each week. On the very first night of my initial shift, as the hour grew late, I was shown to a nearby family room where I could rest. Mrs. Bush then proceeded to turn on several lights, which she explained would make it easier for me if I had to move about during the night. She then retired for the evening. Though she had just met me, her kind thoughtfulness made me feel more like a guest than an employee within the walls of their home.

The next year, Mrs. Bush displayed this same thoughtfulness and concern when several of her visiting grandchildren settled down in the family room to pass the night away watching a movie. Before she retired for the night I heard Mrs. Bush inform them of a change in their plans. "You'll have to watch this movie someplace else. This is Eben's room!" As I recall, the room emptied fairly quickly.

These are just two examples of Mrs. Bush's kindness and compassion shown during my time with this remarkable couple. It was my great honor and pleasure to have been given the chance to work for President and Mrs. Bush. I will remember them with respect and affection for the rest of my life.

– **Eben Worthley** *(left)* **with Tom Putnam and President and Mrs. Bush**

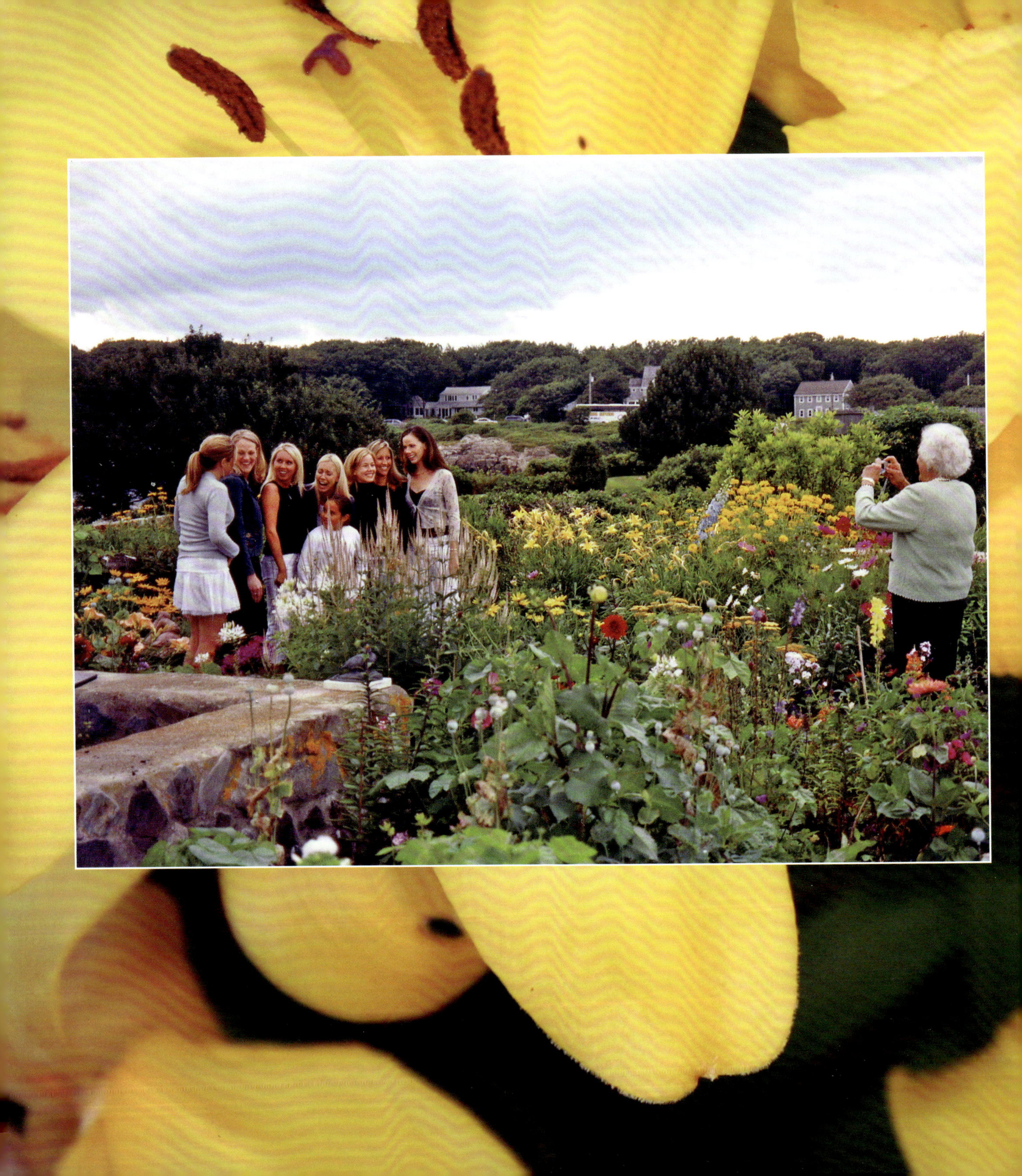

On an August evening in 2004, Ariel De Guzman, President and Mrs. Bush's chief steward, had a bit of a problem. A pre-wedding reception was being held for George P. Bush and his bride to be, Amanda Williams, at Walker's Point and the guest list had grown considerably over the original estimate. Ariel needed some extra help, and so he reached out to several of his friends who owned or operated stores, asking if we might be willing to give him a hand. We all quickly said yes, excited by the prospect of being able to play even a very small part in such a wonderful occasion. As we were setting up, before the guests had arrived, Barbara Bush came by to greet each of us. What's more, she had her familiar camera in hand and summoned over First Lady Laura Bush so that she could take each of our pictures with her. These Barbara would later print out and have Laura sign, so that we would have our own personal memento from the day. With so much going on and with so many friends and family members soon to arrive, we were all struck by her thoughtfulness. We thought we were just the work crew, but Barbara Bush made us feel like family.

– **Tom Bradbury**

Back when my son was very little, we used to go for evening rides on Ocean Avenue, or "The Moon Road" as we called it since it was a great place to see the moon coming up out of the sea. And driving past Walker's Point, we would always say, "There's George's house!" It was a few years later, when Max was in first grade, that he came to realize with great disappointment that the homeowner we were referring to was NOT the familiar storybook character *Curious George*.

Knowing of Mrs. Bush's love of reading, we thought she might like to know the tale, so Max painstakingly wrote out a letter explaining his sadness. She was sweet enough to take the time to write him in response, saying "Dear Max, Thank you for your delightful letter. I had a great laugh. Although I am very fond of Curious George, I am so glad that it's George Bush who lives there. With all best wishes, Warmly, Barbara Bush."

And then, in beautiful handwriting below the typed note, she added, "Sometimes… I think he is a little curious. See you soon."

— Jenne James

In July of 2003 I had the honor of having the President and Mrs. Bush's chief steward, Ariel De Guzman, bake my wedding cake. Because the process took up Ariel's time, not to mention kitchen space and the whole refrigerator, Mrs. Bush made the benevolent decision that she and President Bush must dine out that evening so Ariel could focus his attention on my cake! Thanks to Mrs. Bush's grace and generosity, my wedding cake was a stunning masterpiece and it came with a memory I will cherish forever.

– Rebecca Bradbury Roberts

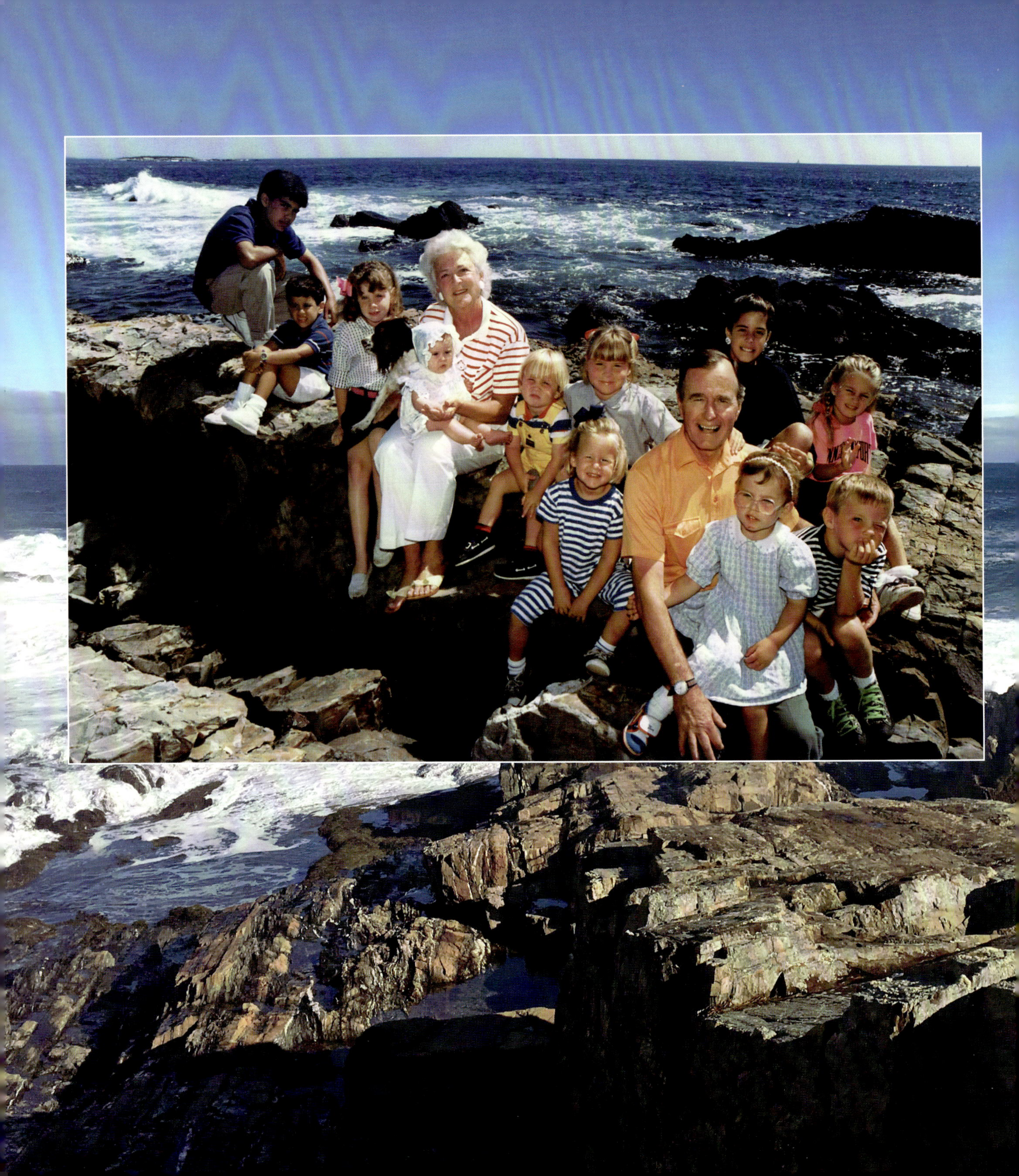

In the early 1980s, while working at Walker's Point restoring the house after the severe storms of those years, my company was doing all the painting. Barbara would stop and talk to each and every one of us. She was truly interested in who we were and what our goals were. Being all in our mid-twenties at the time, it was quite a thrill to be working there and treated so kindly by her. After we all finished in 1978 George and Barbara threw a party for all of the workmen. George was pouring beer from the keg and Barbara was passing out plastic cups with her initials BPB on each one.

One incident occurred while we were painting the entryway. The furniture had just been delivered from Texas and the Secret Service came in with three German shepherd bomb-sniffing dogs. They told us to keep working and stay still. Suddenly out of nowhere came *Millie*, their spaniel, who dove into all three German Shepherds. They finally got them separated, put *Millie* in another room and told us not to tell Barbara, which we didn't. Twenty something years later while I was working for a client, Barbara stopped by to see my client, a friend of hers, and remembered me, so I was able to tell her the story of *Millie* and the shepherds, explaining that I assumed the statute of limitations had run out. She got quite a kick out of the story. She was such a down-to-earth person who treated everyone as an equal. She will be missed and remembered with great admiration. I will always be a better person for knowing her.

– Craig McInnis

My husband, Potentate Dick Bibber, hosted the 1997 Kora Shrine Northeast Summer Ceremonial in Kennebunkport with headquarters at the Colony Hotel. A huge parade was held in Kennebunk with motorized and marching units from Nova Scotia to Rhode Island exciting the crowds on the sidewalk with their maneuvers, music and their clowning skills. A chicken barbecue was held under several tents in Wells. The highlight for us was an invitation from President Bush and Barbara to join them at Walker's Point along with 25 other couples for afternoon refreshments. What a thrill! When we arrived we were greeted by Barbara and she asked the ladies to join her in the family room. The boys could go out on the deck with George. She had many questions about where we were from and how we helped the Shrine children. She seemed pleased that it was all at no cost to the families. After about an hour of enjoying her company and refreshments, she offered to have a photographer take a picture of each couple with her and the President. They were both so gracious and genuinely interested in the number of participants willing to help burned and handicapped children in need. The President then took his boat to Wells Harbor where the majority of Shriners were gathered for a band concert. The Highlanders piped President Bush from his boat to the gazebo where he addressed the crowd. Everyone was so appreciative, especially Dick and me. We have been so blessed to have them both in our lives.

— **Patty Bibber**

I had the great honor of working for Barbara Bush for nearly 30 years, starting at the White House in 1989 as one of her deputy press secretaries. What an adventure that was for a farm girl from Missouri, who didn't even leave the United States of America until she was 30.

Thanks to George and Barbara Bush, I traveled the world, met Kings and Queens, and witnessed history. But mainly, I learned from two of the best people we'll ever know what is most important in life: Faith, family, and friends. The photo at bottom right was taken at the Republican National Convention in 1992, in Houston. (Please note the TV screen behind Mrs. Bush!) I don't remember exactly what I was telling the First Lady, but it was either shocking news or really, really good gossip. Just look at that face! Either way, this photo reminded me of what a wonderful rollercoaster it has been, filled with good times and a few tough ones, but never ever boring.

– Jean Becker

A dinner in Kennebunkport at Walker's Point… Just Bar and George, the four of us and our wives. After dinner Mrs. Bush asked if each one at the table would share a story about their parents and their upbringing; something meaningful that helped mold us into that what we had become. Oh, the stories. Oh, the memories of that intimate time with a former First Lady. All who sat around the table shed tears and it became clear once again why we loved this woman like we did. Who else would do that but Barbara Bush?

Some day we will sit together again, in a place where there is no darkness. And Barbara's light will be one of the brightest there… as she was here! We love you, Barbara Bush.
— Joe Bonsall, Richard Sterban, Duane Allen, and William Lee Golden
THE OAK RIDGE BOYS

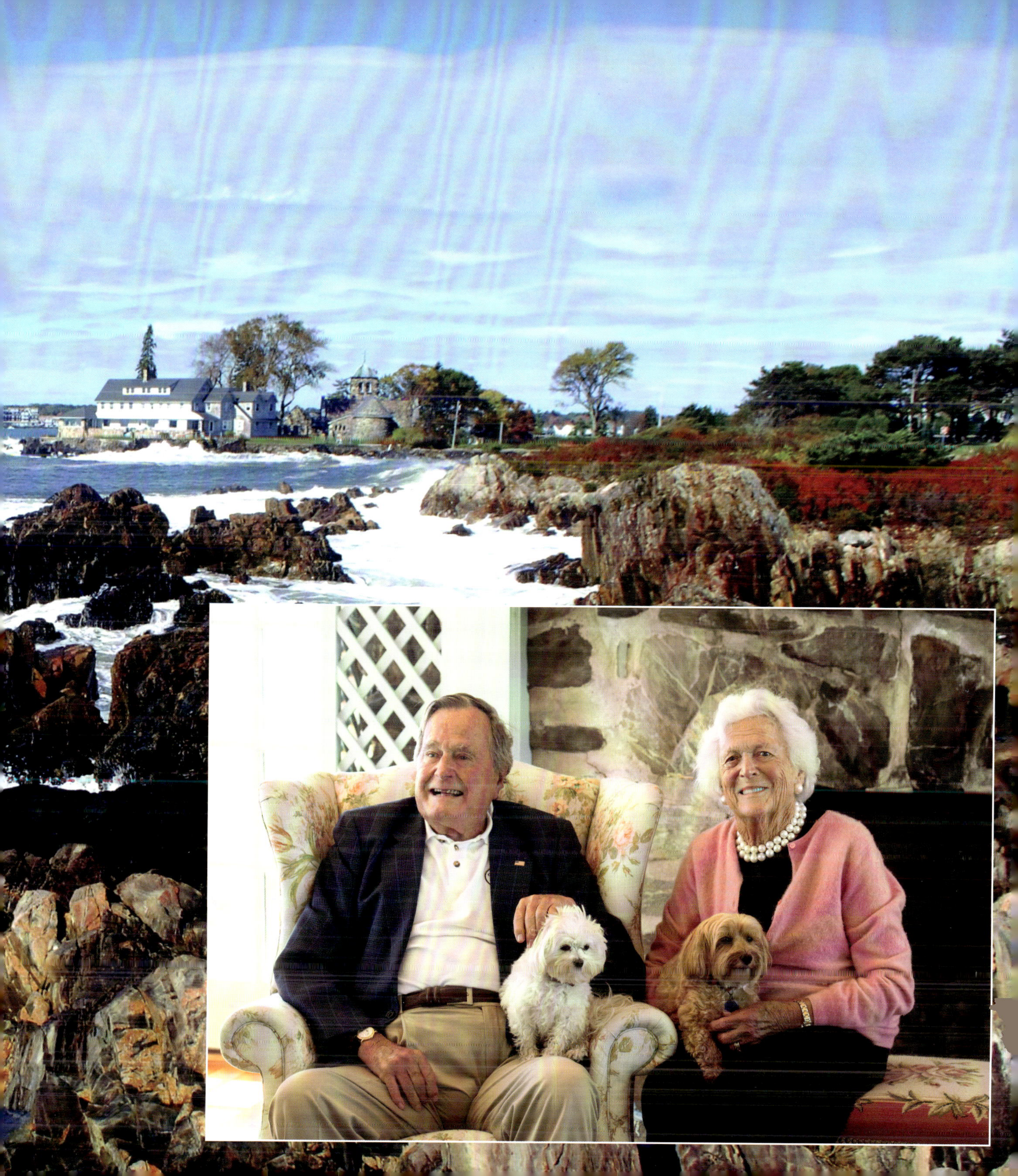

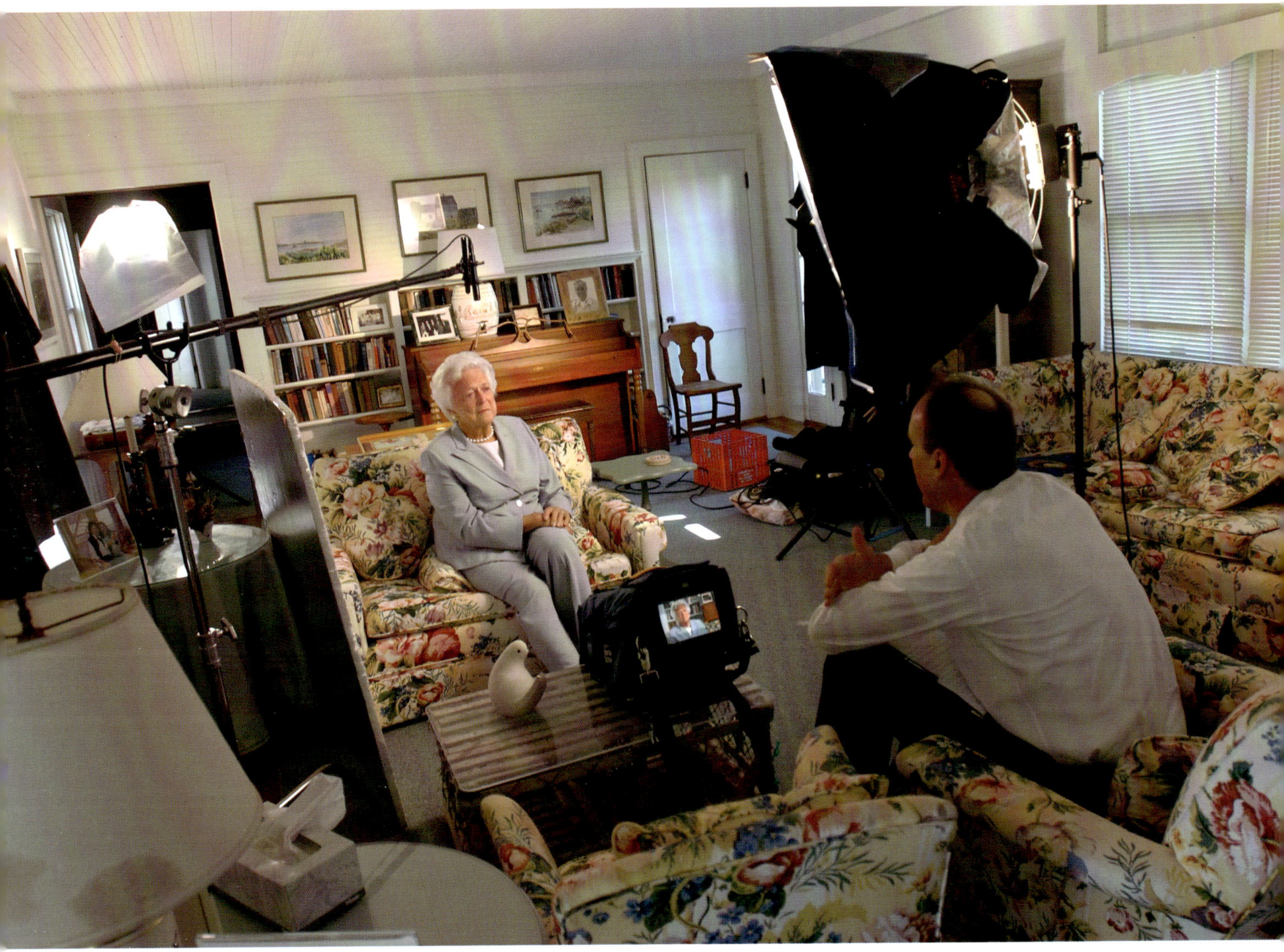

In November 2005, I accompanied a TV production crew to Walker's Point to interview Mrs. Bush. We were there to capture memories of her mother-in-law, Dorothy Walker Bush, for our client, Southern Maine Medical Center, which was dedicating a new emergency care pavilion in honor of her husband's mother. Our crew was given an hour to set up in the bungalow, a single-story shingled cottage immediately adjacent to the Big House. We were told that Mrs. Bush would arrive promptly at the top of the hour for the interview. As you can imagine, we prepared with focus.

About 15 minutes before Mrs. Bush was due to arrive, the director asked me to sit in a small upholstered chair directly across from where Mrs. Bush was to sit so they could adjust lighting, face angles, etc. I carefully sat down…and promptly broke through the webbing of the chair. For a moment I sat there stunned, looking like a grasshopper with my knees up near my ears, until the crew burst into laughter. I was so flabbergasted I couldn't speak. Here I was, about to meet the famed Silver Fox, who was known for speaking her mind. The Secret Service might have code named her "Tranquility" but what would she say about me ruining her furniture?

Because the clock was ticking, and we had to get the crew focused, I stood up, threw some couch pillows into the divot, and sat back down so the crew could finish their lighting. "We'll tell her chief of staff after the interview," I said, feeling a bit sheepish and completely embarrassed.

At the top of hour, right on the mark, in walked Mrs. Bush looking elegant in a beautiful baby blue pantsuit that perfectly complemented her white hair and signature pearls. I gestured to the couch where she was to sit. "Thank you for your time this morning," I said, trying to focus on the task at hand. "I only have a few questions."

"No need, I know exactly what I want to say," she said with clear authority as she turned to sit on the couch.

OK, I thought. I see what people mean about her directness.

When she sat down, she too broke through the couch webbing. It wasn't as dramatic a collapse as mine, but it was certainly noticeable.

"Omigosh, Mrs. Bush," I said as I jumped up to help fish her out. I noticed the crew behind the lights struggling hard not to laugh.

She waved me off. "No problem, don't worry about it. Happens all the time," she said as she stood up, tossed some pillows in the divot and sat back down. She looked right at me and said, "Let's go."

Tranquility indeed.

– Tim Dietz

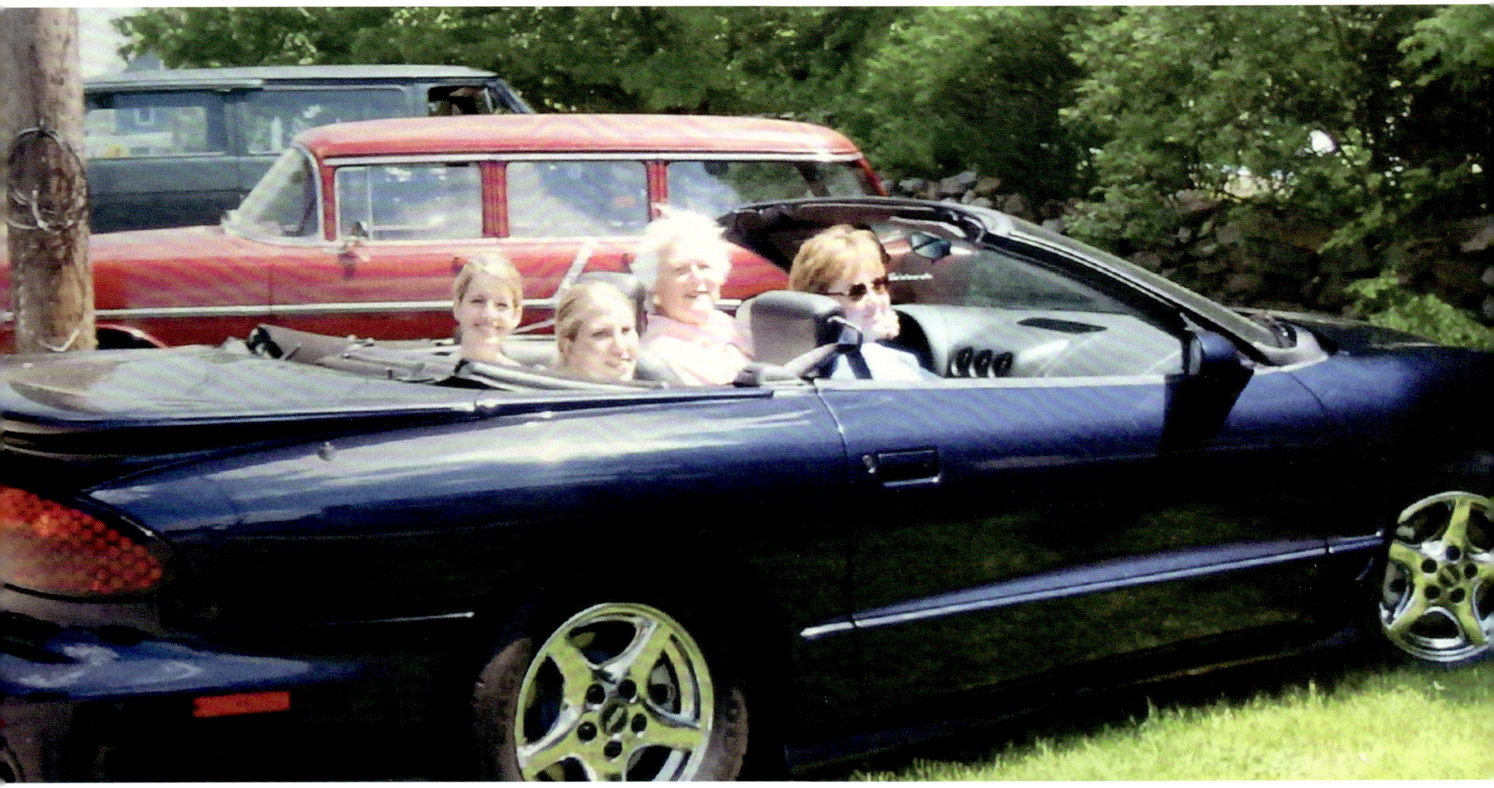

I like statistics. I can't always qualify them and you might not be able to always confirm them, but I am pretty sure that 100% of the people I have ever talked with love Barbara Bush. And I am among them.

Lucky enough to work for her as her post presidency Chief of Staff from 2000 - 2003, I have had many conversations about Mrs. Bush and they all begin with "I love Barbara Bush!" and "What was she like? Is she as great in person? She seems so normal."

Yes and no. Barbara Bush was not normal. She was extraordinary. She was funny and quick and smart and steadfast and loyal and honest (to a fault) and caring and generous and competitive and unflappable and human. And I guess normal. Immediately following her death, it was comforting to discuss and remember the amazing things she did for literacy and cancer and AIDS and beyond. But I personally enjoy stories that show her to be human.

Working at Walker's Point was always exciting. There were family and kids and dogs and visitors galore. At any moment President Bush would ask us to drop everything when he wanted to take us to lunch on the boat. While Mrs. Bush loved being with her husband, in her later years the pounding of the boat on the waves was uncomfortable so she would go by car and meet us at the restaurant. While her mode of transportation changed, her love of Maine endured.

Our work was frequently interrupted when Mrs. Bush announced that she was heading to the golf course, going shopping, or taking the dogs to the beach. She enjoyed the same things in Maine that we all do. One fun summer she had a convertible and would drive us to lunch or to the movies or she would run into town on an errand.

She enjoyed having guests at Walker's Point, which often numbered in the hundreds in any given summer. So she created rules. Make your bed. Hang your wet towels. Guests of guests are not allowed to bring guests. One summer I helped her purchase a basket full of flip-flops so she could encourage the grandchildren to change their sandy shoes as they entered the house. It was a constant flow of people and food and games and memory making.

Mrs. Bush was always on the go, frequently doing those everyday normal things with everyday normal people — all of whom she considered her friends.

– Brooke Sheldon

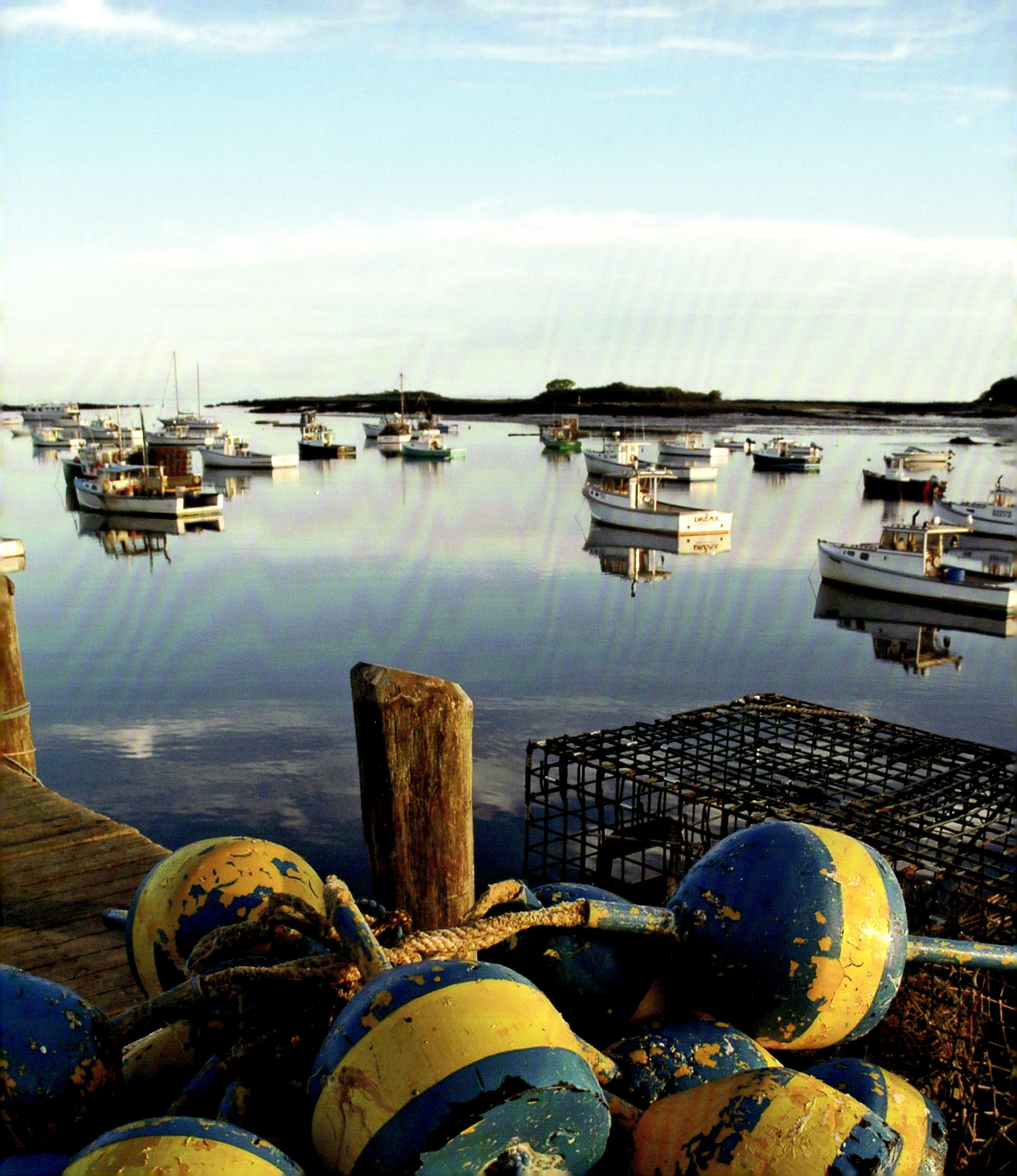

"Would you like to go antiquing with Mrs Bush?" someone casually asked me while I was hanging out in the kitchen at Walker's Point back around 2007.

"Alone?" I responded, feeling somewhat terrified. "Well, there will be Secret Service accompanying you," came the response.

I smile as I remember this story. Mrs. Bush and I ended up having a great time — the first of many such adventures I was honored to share with her and her family and friends over the years. Mrs. Bush had a tough reputation — and she was tough — but there was nothing to be afraid of. She was witty, generous, loving and a woman who easily inspired. I loved to see her with her children, her dogs, in the element of her work with her Literacy Foundation and, of course, with her husband, the President. She was always grateful for my support and for the times I was able to assist her with something small like helping to get her camera flash working.

This photo was from her 90th birthday gala held at St. Ann's in Kennebunkport. I was very nervous to emcee the event because I wanted to deliver a quality performance on the scale of the huge respect and admiration for her I had in my heart. And I had to speak in front of two former Presidents and a lot of other very accomplished folks! It was a wonderful night, one I hope she enjoyed.

I will always treasure the fact that I got to know her in a small way and had the opportunity to serve causes that I know were dear to her.

    – Teri Hatcher

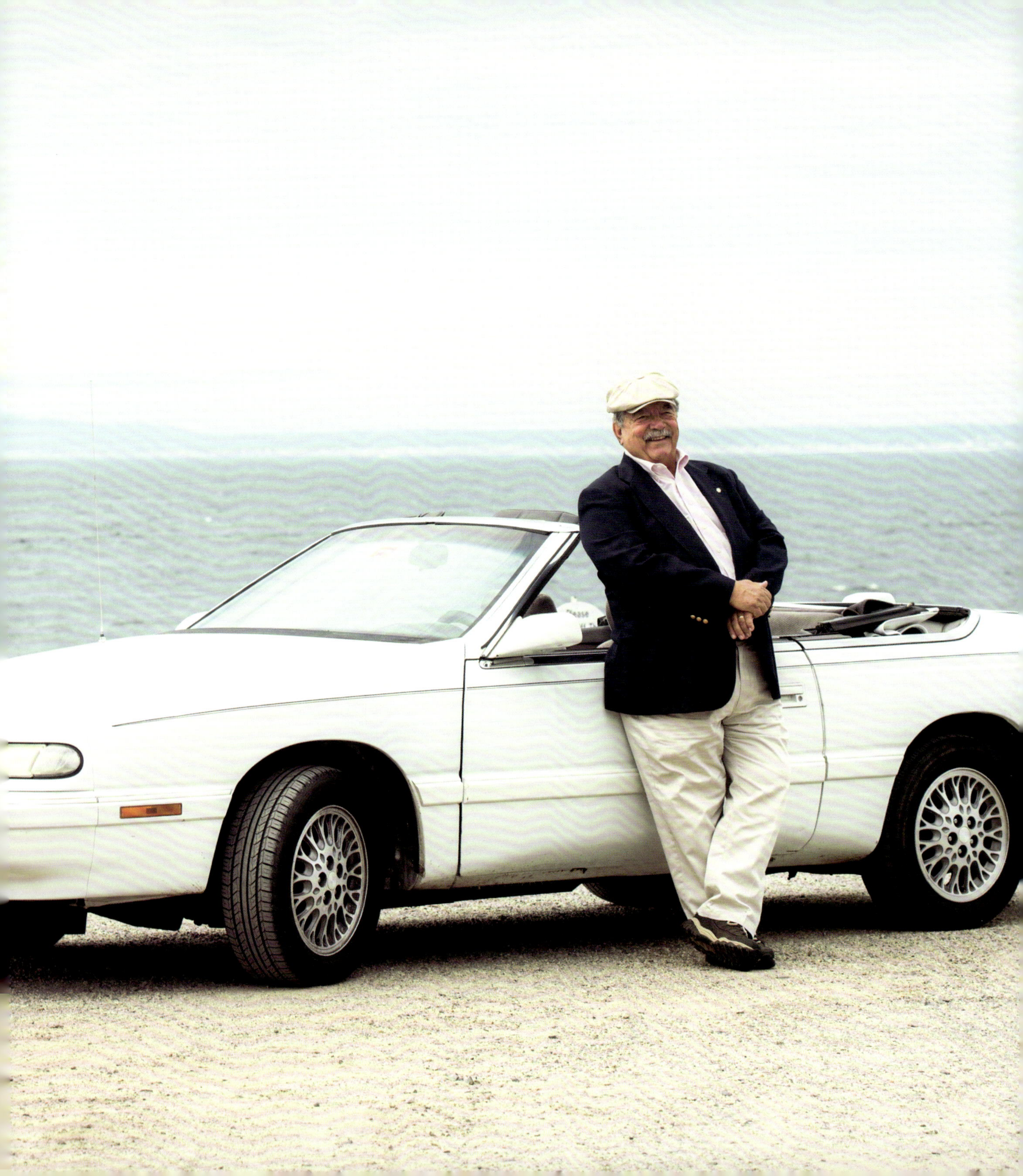

Shortly after President Bush won the election in 1988, I joined a very special group of local volunteers. Our job was to drive one of the Summer White House fleet of rentals in order to make the President's time here safe and comfortable. Each one of us "locals" went through the necessary background checks and were approved by the Secret Service.

One hot summer day I received a call from the switchboard at the "Summer White House" asking me to be at that office at 6:00 p.m. and expect to spend the evening. By 6:15 I was at Government Wharf in Kennebunkport to pick up people being ferried there, as it seems their boats were too big to fit in the river.

After loading everyone into the mini-van, we (the Secret Service and I) headed to Walker's Point. As we drove up to the front door Mrs. Bush and *Millie*, her now famous dog, were there to greet us. Mrs. Bush opened the side door, smiled, hugged each of the passengers and cheerfully stated "George will be right along." After parking out of the way, I settled down with a book for the evening.

About two and half hours had passed when I noticed Mrs. Bush walking toward the car. She had a glass of lemonade and a plate of cookies.

"Hello there!" she said, handing me the drink and cookies. "These are for you with my thanks. We love it when old friends come for the evening, but we couldn't do it without your help."

"Yes Ma'am," I replied, somewhat taken aback by her visit. "Thank you Ma'am." She didn't linger and immediately returned to the house. I sat there drinking lemonade, eating cookies and I thought, "WOW! The First Lady just brought me cookies!"

About 45 minutes later the Secret Service told me to move the mini-van back to the front door to reload my passengers. President and Mrs. Bush walked their guests over to me and shook hands or hugged each one of them. The President came to the driver side window, stuck his hand in and shook mine and said, "Thank you for taking care of my friends." Mrs. Bush added, "Yes, thank you for giving up your evening so that we could see our old friends."

As we drove off I noticed in my rearview mirror that they stood waving until we made the turn onto Ocean Avenue.

– **Steve Adams**

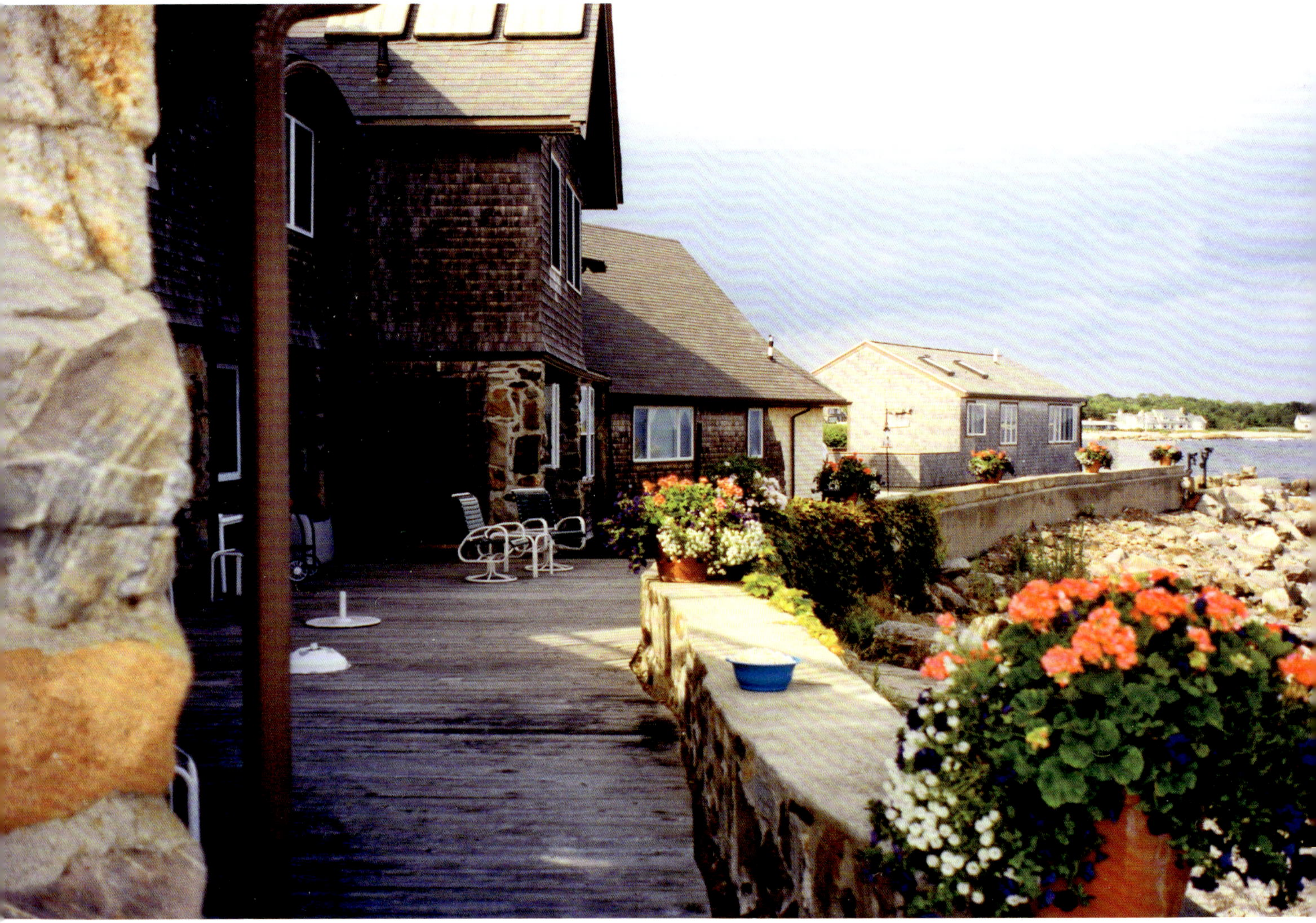

Mrs. Bush became a very dear friend to me over the 15 years I provided massages for the President and Mrs. Bush. The first time I went out to Walker's Point to massage her, and her husband, she talked with me the whole time. She wanted to know all about my daughter. When she found out that Mariah, who was 11 at the time, had taken the babysitters course and was a certified babysitter, she wanted her to babysit for her grandchildren and later, the great grandchildren. Mrs. Bush enjoyed watching my daughter grow up. She would always ask how she was doing and would send her love along to her.

One day after massaging President Bush 41, he invited Mariah and me to join him and "Bar", for dinner at the White Barn Inn, one of the most exclusive restaurants in the Kennebunks. Mrs. Bush thought that was a great idea. Mariah and I had never been there and it was such an honor to join them. It was just the four of us and there was never an uncomfortable moment. Mrs. Bush always made us feel so welcome and comfortable.

Barbara had two dogs, *Mini* and *Bibi*. The dogs typically do not take to people other than their beloved owner and also have a tendency to bite people now and again. Even 41! Most of the relatives and friends who know the dogs are afraid of them and make a point to avoid them. Mrs. Bush couldn't get over how much the dogs loved me. I think giving them treats on a weekly basis helped. She told me that the love her dogs had for me had grown beyond treats. They would get quite excited to see me. I'd pick them up and they would give me kisses. *Mini* had a habit of doing a little twirling dance when she saw me. Once in a while Mrs. Bush would ask that I stop massaging President Bush for a few minutes to show whomever was visiting, whether a relative or a friend, just how much the dogs loved me. I guess I became the *Mini* and *Bibi* whisperer. It was fun to watch the joy it brought her.

Mrs. Bush would sit in her wingback chair and needlepoint beautiful Christmas stockings for her great grandchildren while I massaged the President. She did a lot of needlepoint for charity fundraisers as well. I miss our conversations. I miss her. She was a good friend.

– **Pam Cummings**

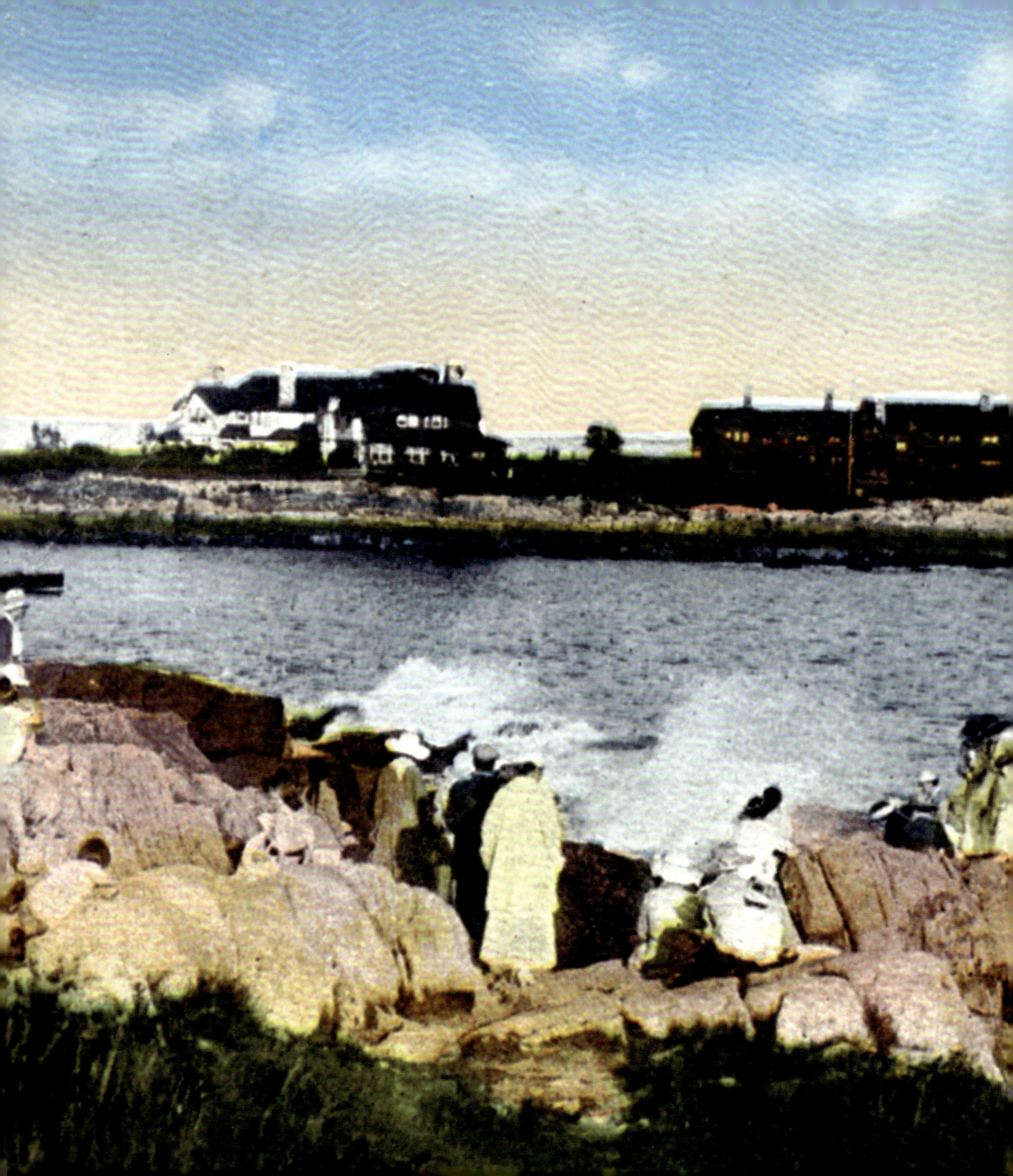

After the purchase of Walker's Point in 1980 from Mary Walker, Bar set to work getting the house ready for her family. It had not been occupied for three years so much work had to be done. One afternoon while Bar was in the house with a helper, Mary Walker, not knowing Bar was there, came over to retrieve some belongings. Bar said to her helper, "Mary Walker. Wonderful lady, but what a mess here." A minute later Mary appeared. Big hugs and kind words followed.

– **Ambassador George "Bert" Walker and Carol Walker**

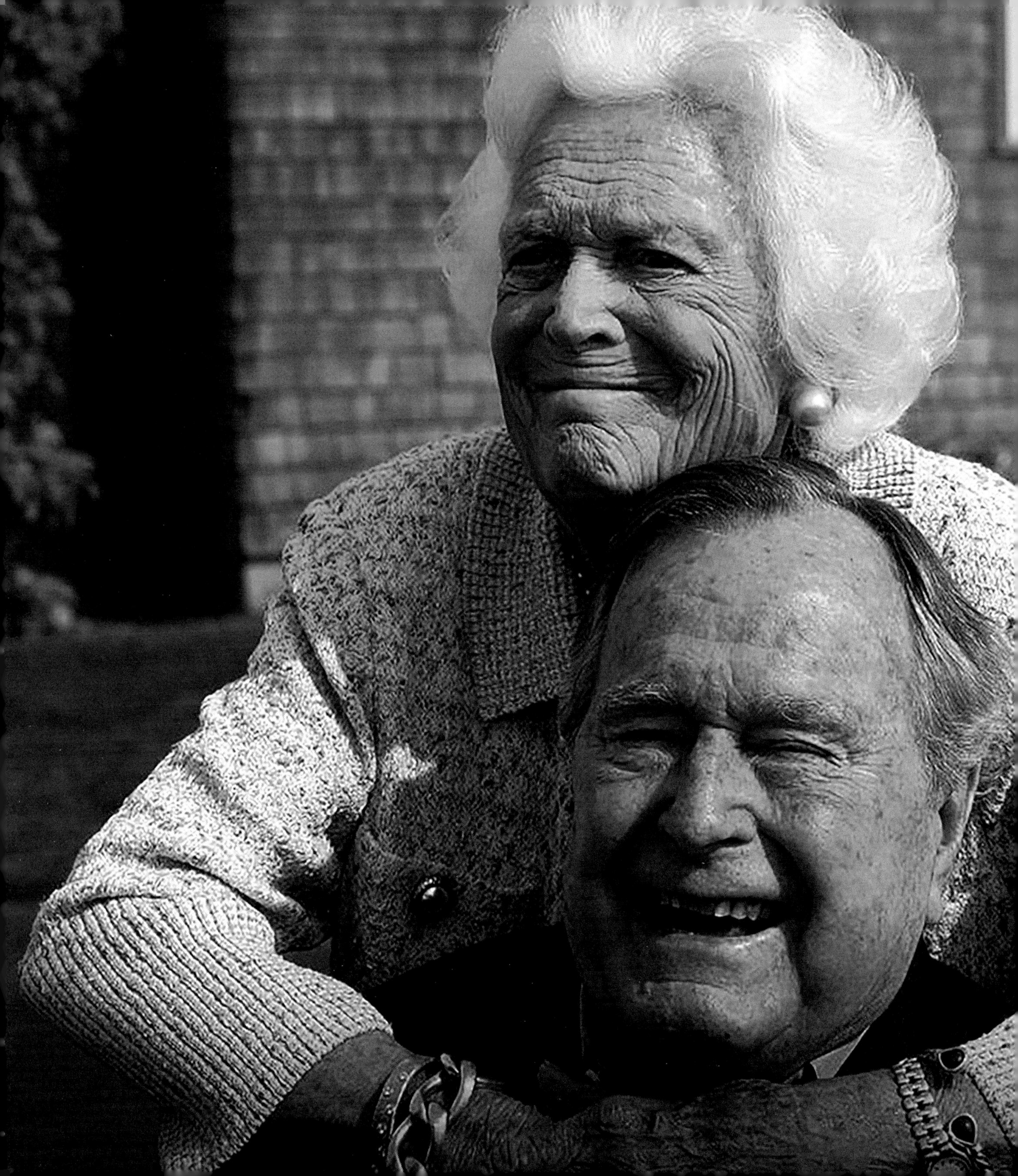

A decade ago, I was on the Washington Mall for the National Book Festival when a woman ran up to me — which doesn't happen enough, believe me. She said, "Oh my God, it's you!" I said, "Well, yes." Hard to argue with that. She said, "Oh, I'm so thrilled to meet you. I so admire you. Will you stay right here while I go buy your book? Will you sign it for me?" I said, "Yes, ma'am," feeling, I must admit, quite full of myself. And then my new female admirer came back — with John Grisham's latest novel.

That had been on a September afternoon, and I was due in Maine the next day to see the 41st president and Mrs. Bush. Feeling sorry for myself, I told them the story. Mrs. Bush shook her head sadly and said: "Well, how do you think poor John Grisham would feel? You know, he's a very handsome man."

So I was 0-2. But it was a fair, funny point — as were so many of the points Barbara Pierce Bush made in her long and consequential life. Known as Barbara, as Bar, as Mom, as Mother, as Ganny, as the Silver Fox, and as the Enforcer, she was candid and comforting, straightforward and steadfast, honest and loving.

Barbara Bush was the First Lady of the Greatest Generation.

– **Jon Meacham**

Just last summer, on their porch in Maine on a sunny day, talk turned to World War II and that terrible Saturday, September 2nd, 1944, when Lt. George H.W. Bush was shot down over Chichi Jima. Two of his crewmates didn't make it, becoming casualties of war. He parachuted out of the bomber, plunged into the sea, came up to the surface, flopped onto his life raft, and waited, scared and retching. Had young Bush been captured by the Japanese, he would have been held captive on an island that was home to horrific war crimes — including cannibalism. ("Bar, I could've been an hors d'oeuvre," he'd say in later years.) It had been the closest of calls. "George," Mrs. Bush said that day in Maine, in their great old age, lost in reminiscence, "you must have been saved for a reason. I know there had to be a reason."

President Bush sat silently for the briefest of moments, then raised that big left hand and pointed his finger across the table at his wife. "You," he said hoarsely. "You were the reason."

— Jon Meacham

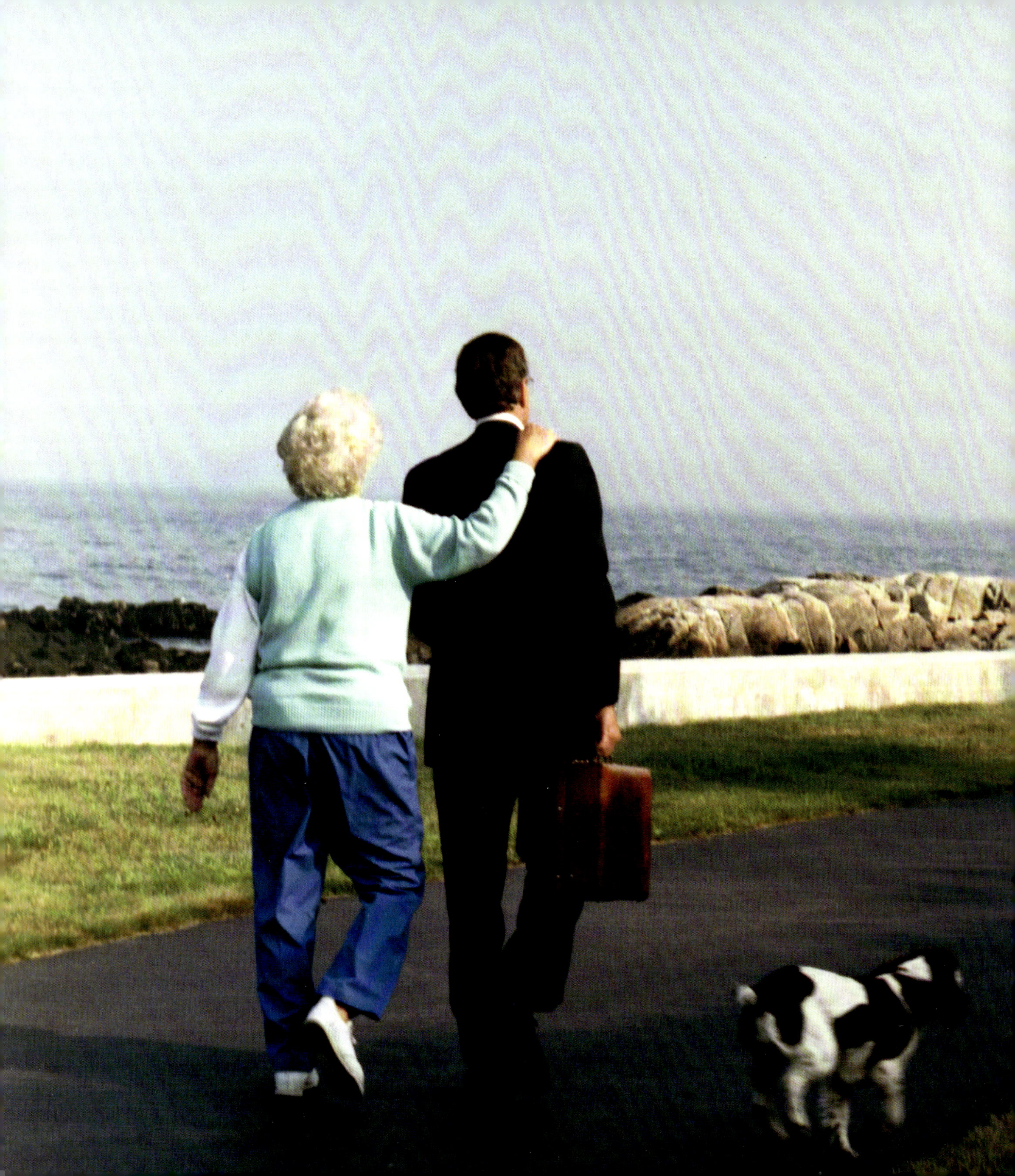

How lucky am I to have been married to the love of my life for more than 73 years.

And what an adventure it was.

We moved from Michigan to Virginia to Connecticut to Texas to California back to Texas to Washington to New York back to Washington to Beijing back to Washington back to Texas back to Washington and then back to Texas to stay.

But our anchor to windward was always Maine, where we came every single year of our married life to recharge our batteries, see old friends and make new ones, and yes, enjoy some lobster and blueberry pie. It was always where the children and grandchildren liked to gather, and where we could be together as a family.

This is one of my favorite photos, taken while I was President and the First Lady met Marine 1 and walked me up the driveway at Walker's Point. Heaven.

As it did then, just breathing in Maine's fresh air restores my soul, never more so than this year.

How lucky I am to call this piece of paradise home.

– **George H.W. Bush**

Photo credits

Tom Bradbury

George Bush Presidential Library and Museum

Robert Dennis

Tim Dietz

Eric Draper

Bill Lord

Jeff Roberts

Chris and Cyndi Smith, CA Smith Photography

If we have missed anyone who contributed a photograph to this publication, we apologize, as we tried to be as thorough as possible in recognizing contributors.

Special thanks to Dietz Associates Inc. in Kennebunk for their coordination and patience in the editing and design of this special publication. We are very grateful for their dedication to helping this book become a reality.

Proceeds from *Our Beloved Barbara: Memories of a Community* will be used to support *Ganny's Garden*, a garden in Kennebunkport, Maine, created to honor and remember Barbara Bush. If you would like to help keep the flowers blooming, contributions can be sent to: *Ganny's Garden*, c/o Kennebunkport Conservation Trust, PO Box 7004, Cape Porpoise, ME 04014.